First Step Toward Ahriman

Copyright 2013 Adam Daniels All rights reserved.

ISBN: 978-1-365-97781-7

Table of Contents

The First Step toward Ahriman is a unique understanding of how religion was brought into the dualistic form. The nature of man was blurred with the divine need for purity. This was created through the lie of a tyrannical subvert that was greedy for power. This "God" named Hormazd was created for the selfish need of Zurvan. It is my opinion that Zurvan was the spark of conscious that made infinite to finite. Thus, Zurvan is the creator of time, otherwise known as Father Time or the Grimm Reaper. This looks into this topic.

As many things throughout history are perverted by the victors, so is the true understanding of the Devil. Rarely has the Devil been given the opportunity to speak for himself. This my friends is now the time. The angelic beings and Hormazd are at war with the demonic beings and Ahriman. This book will give the understanding as to why and give the knowledge to work with freedom away from the tyrannical God that is fattening you up for his consumption. Heaven is the Lake of Fire; Hell is the dark watery abyss of the Earth's Womb. Choose!!!

Who is Father Ahriman?

I guess I have not made this very clear to the public. The reason is simple; to find Ahriman you must study. Wikipedia is very limited with the amount of information it provides about Father Ahriman and His cohorts. I think this is because media doesn't want this information easily accessed. Reason being, it would expose how much of Catholicism was constructed through Zoroastrianism.

Ahriman is the antithesis to Ahura Mazda. Both deities have the ability to create. Ahriman is the twin brother to Ahura Mazda and has similar abilities to affect reality. Ahura Mazda is order, blind faith, and obedience. Ahriman is chaos, questioning, and defiance. In other words, Ahura Mazda wishes to enslave you to his way to earn some after life that is a sham.

Ahriman wishes to free you from slavery and allow living life to its fullest. With that being said, I've been told that I'm sugar coating Ahriman. In a way, to the public eye I am. So, let's remove the veil and the sugar coating; are you prepared for this? Angra Mainyu aka Father Ahriman is an outright destructive force that plagues humanity with vexation, corruption, plague, drought, flood, starvation, sin, war, domination, and etc. He is the antithesis, the embodiment of "Evil." Satan take a step back, daddy is here to play.

As a vicar to Father Ahriman, I've had to do a balancing act which I found through reading Rudolf Steiner's works about "spiritual science." Catholics and the Muslims down played this Devil. Why, because Ahriman has equal power to the God figure.

If holy and evil have equal footing, how can the holy have dominion? That is why Zoroastrianism failed and Christianity and Islam propel forward into the future. They downsized the devil to a rebellious underling that can still be controlled by their power, the true lie. What actually happened to Ahriman and why is he entrapped in a water filled abyss? Ahriman caused so much chaos that after He blotted out the Endless Light, Ahura Mazda and his minions outnumbered Ahriman and imprisoned Him. This did not stop Ahriman, after Mother Jeh roused Him, He turned His gaze unto mankind.

The worst thing that can happen is to get people to apostate from the holy. Whether or not these people join Ahriman's cause it does not matter, so long as they break away from the enslavement. Do realize that Father Ahriman does use the same tools against the holy as he always has. The Daevas, Dews, and Druj are allowed to come onto Earth and influence people by whispering in their ears to create chaos. When you learn to understand what the whispering means, then you can tap into the spiritual plan that is set aside for you.

Do I as a human vicar condone all evil in the world? No. Most of the evil is influence by these denizens of Hell because they need energy to sustain themselves on the mortal plane. Why would they influence murder for example, to feed off the energy that comes from the adrenalin release from the act. Here is the question I ask you, if a person is influenced by said entity to do such a monstrous act, you should question the stability of said person. The reason that these entities attack these unstable people is because these people are the most religiously devout slaves to the holy.

Let us examine this concept. If one constantly denies their animal nature, pressure builds to sate this issue. Breathing is obviously most important and the list of needs goes from there. Without fulfilling these needs, psychological pressure builds and after a point the brain will contort the need into something else from religious teachings. Thus creating a heavy form of conflict in one's being. Most use alcohol to combat pressure and then proceed to fulfill the need. Then feel guilty and return to religion to sate the guilt. Thus the cycle continues.

Now let us look to the devout who never play into the game, but continue to deny them. These folks usually end up on the news or doing weird dangerous acts. This is done by the manipulation of psychological ego defense mechanisms either internal or spiritual. These are the folks that the entities love to whisper to. The Ahrimani entities are aggressive in nature and can provoke quite a reaction out of somebody.

They are trying to free this person from enslavement, but the person keeps fighting and contorts more till some type of destructive act occurs, freeing the individual. That may come in the form of suicide, murder, or other heinous acts. These acts are considered evil and evil inspired, but the reality of it is, fighting the holy fight drives them into madness and evil.

If you learn to accept your animal nature and use it as tool, and learn to whisper back, wonderful changes can occur in your life. Learn to work with "evil" and you will wield power, fight with evil and it will wield power over you. Don't become a spiritual or religious victim because the "holy law is such." You decide by your own defined morality how far down the rabbit hole you will go and celebrate being a natural creature of the Earth that has attuned with the original denizens of Hell!

Beginning of Time

Purusha is a being of 1,000 heads, 1,000 eyes, and 1,000 feet. It is the essence of the Universe. The other name of this essence is Khwaskhwarrik, the "mother" of the twin sons, Hormazd and Ahriman. From this a light of consciousness sparked into the universe known as Zurvan, the beginning of Time. The Infinite became Finite because of Zurvan's existence.

Zurvan had an overwhelming need to have a son named Hormazd. Through this need, Zurvan began to sacrifice the essence, Purusha. Through 1,000 sacrifices, the Daevas were created, and Zurvan was unaware. During these thousand sacrifices Zurvan began to build doubt. This was the self-conscious doubt that all his effort was in vain because there was no sign of change.

Within the womb of Khwaskhwarrik developed the son known as Hormazd and through Zurvan's insecurity of doubt, Ahriman became fruit within the womb as well. Over time both twin Gods developed within the essence of the Universe. Outside Zurvan became excited as Daeva Nanshait (Shiva) made Zurvan aware of the twins. Nanshait convinced Zurvan to decree that the 1st son by his side would receive the kingdom. So it was so decreed.

Daeva Nanshait was able to communicate with Ahriman through the womb. Nanshait informed Ahriman of Zurvan's decree. This vexed Ahriman into action. At this point in Time

9

Ahriman was unaware of Hormazd. Now with this new understanding of both the decree and the race to Zurvan, Ahriman had to act fast.

Creation

When I became self-aware, all was darkness. Complete stillness within a black chasm filled in a watery base. Throughout my time within I would bump into another who was like me, but not yet self-aware. I did not know that was my brother, let alone my sworn enemy at that time. If only I'd known then, I would have destroyed him.

As things developed, I began to hear exterior noises, and over time I began to understand these noises. My brother did become self-aware, and also understood the noises. While he rested, I heard the noise say, "I will grant my favor to whom is born first." In my mind I saw my father, Zurvan! That motherfucker promised favor over everything to the first born.

There was also another voice who spoke to me, and he called himself Nanshait. He explained to me what that meant. He also explained that if I didn't find my own way out, my chances were slim. The lesson of creating my own was learned before birth. I hold Arch-Daeva Nanshait above all others. This is why.

Then I moved about, bouncing off everything to find a way out, of my own mother. There was no way! I became desperate, I wanted to appease and attain favor! The walls felt pliable, so I grabbed and clawed at them. Shuttering began, other noises followed and I attained a greater focus and determination than I ever did; a joy of triumph.

At the time, I was unaware of what was happening to my mother or even what she was. I kept tearing and clawing into the pliable solid, and felt a surge of energy and desperation. I took in this energy and it elated and drove me to continue to my goal. My intended focus became sharp and precise. My surroundings were shuddering, and noises of pain pushed my energy levels to a cataclysmic push!

I remember as I tore through the threshold of her flesh, a huge burst of my energy and her essence slung into the void. As I pulled myself out, my father Zurvan grabbed me by the throat. He looked me over and said, "Thou art dark and stinky! You are not my son!" "Zurvan, did he not just abort himself to fulfill your decree? Does he not get your favor and kingdom?" asked Nanshait.

I stared at Zurvan, my gaze pierced his mind. The fear took over him; this again spiked my energy level. This was an uncontrollable rush. I started shaking and became jittery. This drove Zurvan's fear even more. Then he threw me into the void and said, "For you have destroyed the essence, you shall rule alone."

So I ended up in some dark recesses of the universe. It seemed to me, as I tore my way out, the husk that I was in exploded. All the pieces turned into what is known as stars, planets, and galaxies. Enraged, I moved toward a planet. I held it between my hands. Then I crushed it.

Pieces of it floated around me. I looked over the pieces. One reminded me of Zurvan. I grabbed that piece, my rage lit up the rock. I threw it, and a comet was made. My shiny hate rock was used to cause more destruction. Looking around, I saw that planets circled around a star. Interested, I floated over to the star. It was a ball of fire beyond what I have seen. I touched it, and it was like a pliable solid of the husk. I wondered if I could manipulate this like I manipulated the planet.

I put my hands around it like before. Again, I used my rage and pushed my energy into the star. The star expanded till it exploded. The fire and energy was enveloping and over vast area around me. The planets and all things around me were destroyed. It energized me and I laughed.

Then just as the energy exploded out it then imploded into a swirl. This black hole acted as a vacuum to the pieces to all that exploded. I grabbed another rock that floated by. I charged it with my rage and threw it into the hole. The rock flew in and disappeared.

Curiously I put my head into the hole all I saw was darkness unharvest. This was mine; I created it, the darkness undefiled by light. I entered into the all-consuming hole, and I knew and felt that both father and brother would never see me here. From here I could watch the actions of my brother. That fucker created light that contained both Endless Form and Endless light. He was harnessing pieces of the husk to create something.

What was it, a planet the revolved around a star he had blessed? On this planet were living creatures that he made by harnessing order of the universe. I wanted this Endless Light and Form. I left the darkness and made my way to this Earth. Before I could come back out, I felt a hand on my shoulder. Nanshait's voices rang out saying, "Wait, Father it's not what you may think it is. That light is your brother, and he is afraid of your power. This is your domain, and we are here with you."

I looked back behind me and saw Nanshait and beyond was about 30 to 40 others with him. They held both male and female gender, and all had their own unique ability of themselves. These where my creations as well, and the dark odorous stench of my hand had corrupted them as I was corrupted. They were made from the same doubt I was.

The original denizens of my domain, known as Hell, and I honor each of them.

"Nanshait, what is that my brother fears?"

"Father, Zurvan made infinity into finite by creating Hormazd. His long bout of scarifies created doubt, thus creating you. Your forced birth created all that is before you, to include our brethren here. Know that your destructive chaotic means influences all things as does Hormazd's compulsion to make all into order. You Father are the antithesis to the finite. Only you hold the power to destroy Hormazd. Understand that everything that Hormazd creates requires parts of his own essence, and all that fall under Hormazd's dominion will be consumed to replace his essences. All that you create will become through the destruction of Hormazd's creation, and your essence is never sacrificed or diluted."

"So it is my task to undo what my Father and Brother have done. I hear them conspiring against me and I know with division over time they shall be conquered. We, all of us shall leave here and undo what they have done. Zurvan may have power to control; we have power to undo this. They conspired war over me; let us take the war to them first."

All my Daeva looked at me and knew I spoke the truth, as I held the rod of wisdom. Skin of blue set ablaze amongst them, the internal heat of the Gods burned brightly throughout our realm. The Black Flame of Wisdom beaconed from my rod,

14

and it burned just as brightly. Deep in the chasm were all sorts of creatures that warmed up to each Daeva, and they now had their own legion of Dew and Druj. Our family stood together and we all knew what had to be done. "Go forth and let us do what has to be done!"

The Confrontation

As we pierced the veil back into the universe, Father and Brother knew. We disrupted the order that was being created, and it was stiffening and stifling. We could move about but our minds felt condensed and I felt this weird tingle that wasn't there before. It was the Endless Light, it penetrated all things. Hormazd had created a way to become omnipresent through the light. Where was this coming from and how do we combat it, I questioned myself.

Some spinning sensation occurred and we stood before Zurvan and Hormazd. They had an additional one with them, that fucking light, Mithra. My hatred began then and there for that penetrating light bearer. Suarva rushed toward Mithra and it took both Nanshait and me to stop him. I kissed Suarva on the forehead and thanked him, but we had to hear the enemy out first.

"Control your dogs, the corrupted are not welcome," Yelled Hormazd!

"Turn off your light bearer and I'm sure you won't get such a violent reaction. We are enraged by your blinding light that penetrates all in this realm to include our thoughts and will. This hatred will be your undoing," I popped off curtly.

Zurvan used his right hand to close the eyes of Mithra. The oppression had been lifted, and all could assume themselves freely again. Zurvan grinned as he looked over to me. My Father knew damn well what he had created with that Mithra. I swore to myself that I will have that killed and dismounted before Zurvan's very feet. I'm the lord of oppression, and not one of mine has a power like that.

"Ahriman I know damn well that you are aware of what is happening, which is why you brought all here with you. The Kingdom belongs to Hormazd, and you created your own realm.

Now I change all. All shall rest in the microcosm of the realm that will belong to man. Just as all of you are of Free Mind, so will man and he shall have free will. Man will have to choose between order and chaos and all shall be bound to this. Whichever one of you who can harvest the most souls of man shall have my favor and the kingdom." Thus spoke Zurvan.

"Are you serious? The game is a harvesting of souls? Fear me you do indeed, rather play games than fight," I tried to reason what Zurvan had said.

Hormazd and Zurvan looked at one another; both had vile grins on their faces. The two fools had no clue I could read and feel their emotions. Smug bastards thought they had a fool proof plan. Looking deeper into Zurvan, I see his fear. He feared his own destruction, and it would only come if finite became infinite again; that would only happen if Hormazd understood doubt.

If Hormazd knew darkness we would both explode and set everything back to nothingness. I question whether or not if consciousness is worth this game?

Looking into the eyes of Father, I called him out, "Father, why don't Hormazd and I embrace on the game?"

"Absolutely not, you vile being of corruption, you stay where you're at. This will be done the way I say it will be. You are unworthy to be with us who are of purity and righteousness," Zurvan proclaimed like a bitch.

"Fear me then, I will play your twisted game. Just know that I will meet you again with a weapon that will kill even fate itself," I said as calmly as I could.

Zurvan pointed to what is known as Earth with his left hand and uncovered Mithra's eyes with his right hand. Then another figured appeared, Varuna. The Endless Light and the Endless Form came together to create this blue egg made of some crystal. I laughed at that display of power. I turned and looked at Nanshait, then asked, "This is what we are to attack?"

We attacked this spirit of the sky. We continued to chip away at this crystalline exterior. Eventually it gave way and had to become bountiful, thus water and the atmosphere was created through my destruction. Land rose up out of the water, and grandest mountain that sought commune with the sky, Alburz a holy place for mortals the fools thought that the universe centered itself here to rotate. Over time the first plants grew, one tree in particular the Saena Tree. This plant created all types of seeds to all types of plants.

In this tree was a bird. This bastard called Saena spread the seeds of this all plant. I have never seen then nor since a creation that shat on everything. They don't tell you that their seed spreader was a bird that was full of shit. I was amused and left it alone.

Then that fucker Mithra created that white bull which ate of the Gaokerena plant. I had some plans for that luminous reflection of light. Just to mock Mithra, I snatched up the bull and took it into the sky. All the way to moon, where I ripped it opened from asshole to mouth. I then sprinkled its guts all over the Earth, laughing the entire time, alas many more plants and animals grew from its entrails.

Finally, as promised, the first man appeared before me on the bank of the River Veh Daiti. I laughed at this ox looking man. It was luminous like the bull. Real hard to figure out whom made this; taking on the form of the serpent I made my way over to it. I lay for a while watching this pious creation.

Shifting back into the form of a young beautiful man, I tapped this glowing ass on its shoulder. Mocking it, I asked for its name. The thing was so stupid, it couldn't even answer. It was as wide as it was tall, and I named it Gayomard the Bumbler. I smacked it in the face and got no reaction; out of pure pity I killed the creature. Soon, the fun will begin because I have harvested the first and only soul.

I stood over this dead body and a large fly approached it. It bowed before me and said, "I am Nasu, the druj of the dead. It is my job to corrupt the body and the soul of the dead. I see Father has already harvested the soul, may I harvest the husk?"

"No, let its creators see what I did to it. This is blasphemy; this man was nothing more than a mobile moron. Let that shitty bird clean up this mess," I replied.

No sooner than I spoke those words, guess who decides to show his fat fucking face again. The sky split and the trumpets sounded, here comes the pious asshole Hormazd. When he saw the corpse of Gayomard, tears filled his eyes. The joy I felt in seeing his sorrow was immeasurable. He looked up at me, and saw my shit eaten grin.

As one tear fell from Hormazd's right eye, an eagle had flown from the tear. Hormazd wailed, "Can you create something good?"

I looked over to Nasu and winked. Nasu quickly rounded up the eagle and brought it to me. From Hormazd's left eye, another tear fell and I caught it.

With his tear in my hand, I charged the eagle as I charged the star. The eagle exploded, and beautiful Melek Taus was created. He stood before us, proud and I said, "I could, but I choose not to!"

"Will you bow down before man, whom I have created? Will you give way to those with a soul?" Hormazd begged Melek Taus.

Melek Taus turned to me, then back to Hormazd and responded, "I am a divine child created from your sorrow and the doubt that is Father Ahriman. I am the smokeless flame of compassion and wisdom. Only through sorrow is wisdom attained; only through wisdom is compassion understood. You seek enslavement upon these souls; Father Ahriman seeks to free them through destruction. I am both divine and damned, and I choose compassion for the souls of man.

I choose Father Ahriman, just as all creatures of this world have choice. We shall meet again Hormazd. Soon, yes soon!"

The look that my peacock had inspired upon Hormazd's face was as wonderful as the tears that fell. My brother's eyes glazed and his jawed dropped agape. Shock had over taken his mind. Fear and doubt ensued into consciousness. He reeked of Zurvan when I ripped my way out.

"Ahriman, you who are foul and corrupted will be defeated in the last age! I will win this war without fail, and I will use the Endless Fire to burn you out of this world!!!" Hormazd yelled.

"Strong words from the weak. Can you not see how much all this creating is weakening you? So bring it, bring your war and I will destroy everything that you throw at me, change its essence then send it back at you. Every time this happens, I gain souls and weaken your joke." I responded in kind.

Mankind

We hung around waiting for something to happen. There is only so much that can happen with a world full of lesser intelligence. Then one morning I saw that shitty bird flying around in a circle, and I remember that being the spot I killed that Gayomard creature. Something was happening, and I had to find out. I assumed the form of Lion to get there quicker.

That shitty bird kept fertilizing the husk of Gayomard. Out of that husk was a rhubarb plant had grown. Its 15 leaves over 15 years produced a conjoined being from the Earth itself. The plant was the being, the being changed from plant to flesh. Then Hormazd came down, he breathed into the form and it became alive. The being became two beings that were alike.

When they became conscious, alive, and aware; Hormazd spoke his righteous lie to them, "You are man, you are the ancestry of the world, and you are created in perfect devotion to me; perform devoutly the duty of the law; which is good thought, good speech, and good actions. Never worship demons."

Hormazd then left them to the world, to me. I walked over to them in the form of a lion. Majestic and beautiful, they became frightened of me. I quickly assumed the form of a beautiful young man. I was able to convince them that I was their creator and that they should worship me. I taught them about corruption and how to be creatures of their own devices.

They became my children of corruption and I named them Mashay and Mashyanag.

Their first lesson was evil speech to be spoken for all to hear. This evil speech drives the will of the Daevas. This evil speech also empowers to me. This is also known as blasphemy and it makes mankind free of enslavement. These words will separate you from Hormazd, the strongest corruption, and when Mashay and Mashyanag exclaimed that I was the creator of all things. They separated from Hormazd; their soul's resting with me in Hell.

These humans got cold and clothed themselves with plants and they got hungry. They wondered off into the wilderness to feed themselves because freedom brings responsibility. They wondered upon a white-haired goat. Both sucked milk out of its utters, and more evil speech was uttered afterward. This empowered the Daevas, and made all food bland. Mashay said to Mashyanag, "My delight was owing to it when I had not devoured the milk, and my delight is more delightful now when it is devoured by my vile body."

They were on their own, and as a serpent I continued to watch.

Hormazd couldn't detect me and sent his Ahuras (angels.) These watchers as I call them, taught my children to create fire, gather, and hunt. Then the sick sons of bitches, taught them to commit animal sacrifice. They took a sheep and slaughtered it, then dropped 3 pieces of meat in the fire. To the dog, (ashra) was fed meat, and a Mashay threw a piece into the air and said, "This is the share for the Ahuras." A vulture (ashra) caught the meat and accepted the sacrifice.

Over time the Ahuras taught them how to create clothing from woven animal skin in the wilderness. Then Mashay dug out a pit and found iron. The Ahuras taught him to pound the iron with a stone. Then Mashay was taught to put an edge to iron. With this blade, they cut wood and were taught to make shelter. At root, my children were still damned and the druj reminded them of this.

In their dreams, the druj shouted from the darkness, "You are man; worship your Father Ahriman! So that your animal nature may repose!" The druj showed Mashay in his dreams what to do next. The premonition was given.

My druj successfully vexed Mashay into action proper. He milked cow and put its milk into a chalice. He prepared the first ritual to receive my blessing. During the bright moonlight, both of my children disrobed back to their primal state. They were quite unrefined, but did me proud. Mashay started the fire as instructed by the angel.

In front of the fire, the druj surrounded them. As the druj gathered, they whispered in the subconscious of the couple. Concupiscence was my essence and now it will become theirs. Mashay held up the chalice and said, "O' Angra Mainyu, Creator of this world and myself. I blaspheme the Ahuras and Hormazd with these evil actions!" Mashay then threw the milk of the cow to the northern quarter where Arezura (Hell Mouth) is based.

The heat of the fire warmed the couple and Mashay turned to Mashyanag and said, "When I see your nakedness, my cock arises and I yearn for you." Mashyanag looked him in the eye and said, "Mashay, when I see your great desire I am also agitated." With this the lesson of Evil Action was learned, and they relieved each other's concupiscence. There is no greater satisfaction to free you from building desire, because the pious said it was evil, yes indulgence to your desire is corruption.

After nine months, Mashyanag brought twins into this world. This indeed was a great moment to free man by having him commit the most heinous actions that were completely against nature and the righteous themselves.

Once the twins were born, I slithered into the camp. I taught them that sometimes, babies are born with problems that could not be resolved over time. These children should be removed, as they will only be a hindrance. The best way to discard them would be to eat them and retain their essence for the next ones, and they listened.

Melek Taus and I had conversed over the conundrum of the propagation of human kind. Melek Taus made a huge point as we noticed more and more Ahuras surrounding over these humans. I knew it would only be a matter of time before these humans would give birth once again, and I knew those damn Ahuras would butt in. We needed a way to maintain the corruption amongst them. Next thing that happened without our understanding, a new female walked into the camp.

We sat back and watched, and it had that same luminous glow as Gayomard and that bull. Zariz jumped to attack, but I had to quell my Daeva of corruption. Let us watch and see. I called forth Melek Taus because that being of light wouldn't be able to smell the corruption on him.

The couple was in obvious shock to see another human. The woman approached them with grace and said, "I am Jahi and the Ahuras are confused as to why the babies were eaten." They looked at one another and Mashay responded, "Those babies were sick and we needed to keep their essence to make healthy ones. The creator taught us this. He is a great Father to us."

Jahi was without clothing and Mashay continued to look upon her nakedness. Mashyanag also noticed Jahi's nakedness, and both members of the couple felt the rise of lust. Jahi could feel the emotion of concupiscence radiating off both of them. Jahi was well aware of she was sent in for, and began kissing Mashyanag. The three engaged in releasing the pent-up desire.

They continued to embrace one another and sometimes it would be just the women. Then other times the man with the woman independently. The inevitable happened yet again, Mashyanag became with child. Jahi was without and didn't understand why. She ran off into the wilderness to be alone.

Jahi was alone and sobbing over being barren. Melek Taus descended from the sky with beauty and grace. "My lady, why is it that you are sad?" Jahi became mesmerized by his beauty, and explained all that had happened. Melek Taus understood why Jahi did not bear youth.

Melek Taus knew that Jahi was a spiritual being born of the physical. They both could physically interact with the physical and spiritual. They were made of both, and veil allowed them threw. As they were of the physical, concupiscence was bread into nature as well. They coupled, creating daughters that could carry the seed of a spiritual or physical being, thus the beginning of my plan.

Once this task was completed, Melek Taus had yet another task to handle before Mashyanag gave birth yet again. Melek Taus presented himself to the couple, and explained that he was the Prince of this world. The creator had a little game for them. Let's see whose seed is the most vibrant. Melek Taus had them both masturbate and collect their fluids in separate vases.

Both were instructed to seal the jars and mark them with a seal to identify which one was whose. They then buried the sealed jars as instructed. "We shall unearth these jars after birth of your children. See if any more offspring should come of this," Melek Taus explained to the couple. They agreed without hesitation.

Melek Taus found Jahi wandering around in the Alburz Mountains. "My lady you wander here," asked Melek Taus. "At night, I see the druj leave this area and return during the day," Jahi responded. "Oh, do you wish to meet the creator," Melek Taus asked with the giddiest grin. "Yes, I would love meet Him," Jahi responded with lust in her eyes. Melek Taus took Jahi through Arezura and brought her to me.

"Father Ahriman, I bring onto you Jahi, luminous female of the camp," Melek Taus announced to me. "Yes, Jahi, why have you sought me out?" I asked. "I see the druj leave here at night and return during the day. They speak of you. I wanted know who you are." Jahi responded. "You have fulfilled your purpose by birthing those daughters." I responded.

Jahi looked into my eyes and said, "Can I not have another purpose. Is there not more to you than your plans?" "Why do my plans concern you, as you have fulfilled your purposed and have been blessed with concupiscence," I asked. "Do you not wish to sate your desire," Jahi asked in a husky tone.

Not knowing what Jahi was asking, I released my desire onto and into her. I was well aware of some type of creation would come forth from this act, but I was aware of what would come of this. My son came of this, and he is only referred to as the black demon. A creature that can lurk invisibly in any shadow or shade, the king killer is what he will become. The Endless Dark creates many weapons.

Mashyanag finally gave birth to another set of twins, and as I thought, that shitty bird came to collect the babies. The shitty bird carried off the babies and Mashyanag began to cry. I took her to the sealed jars. She unearthed the jars and opened hers first. It was barren. She looked up at me with pain I could barely endure, so reached down and pulled the other jar out of the ground. I opened it for her, inside was another set of twins.

Elation took over Mashyanag and she now understood that Hormazd and the Ahuras were about pain and blood. Holding her babies I spoke to her, "I told you to keep the other babies' essence until healthy ones could be born. Here they are born of the Earth without pain and blood. Ecstasy of the self, created these powerful children. Soon you will see what happens with the other children who will be guided by Hormazd and the Ahuras. Yes, much blood and pain. These children shall be known as the Sons of Adam, and they will always have my blessing."

Propagation

I left them to see where that shitty bird took the other babies. Not to my surprise, that shitty bird took them back to the Saena Tree that was in the middle of the Vourukasha Sea. I called a swarm of toads to attack the roots of the tree. Of course there was a huge fish called Kara, it ate the toads. There was the Righteous Ass; 1 golden horn, 3 legs, 6 eyes, and 9 mouths.

Jahi brought me a creature as I stood on the bank of Vourukasha Sea. It came from one of her daughters who fucked an Ahura. It was an Azhi (dragon), its heels were golden. I fed it and it quickly grew huge. I named it Gandareva, and left it to terrorize the Righteous Ass and the shitty bird.

While Gandareva was harassing the Righteous Ass, 3 Ahura watchers stood over the shitty bird. The shitty bird nursed the babies till the watchers could take over. The same ones as before: Spenta Armaiti, Kshathra Vairya, and Ameretat. Spenta Armaiti taught animal sacrifice, Kshathra Vairya taught shelter, and Ameretat taught tools. Hormazd's most trusted Amesha Spentas (Arch-Angels.)

Two types of man developed over time, the ones taught by Amesha Spentas and the ones taught by the Arch-Daevas. The righteous ashavans and the wicked drugvants were the two types of man. Those born with a blessing were known as Magi and Yatus. These were the wise men and sorcerers; these people were able to communicate with the spiritual entities. They are the ones who melded reality through the power of the spirit.

As man propagated the 7 lands, chaos broke loose. Ahuras and Daevas were fucking the daughters of Jahi. Divs, Ahzis, and Magic birds were created. The Divs were headed up by Div-e Spenta (White demon.) Divs were demons that where harry and ape like. Some called them giants and since they were abominations they attacked everything.

Dragons attacked men and beasts of burden. The Magic Birds were fickle, never knew which way they go, order or chaos. The Divs would fuck or rape women and create another creature, heroic men. These people were fickle because they had free will to choose sides. The pious remained righteous and the sinister remained wicked.

War broke out amongst all. Heroes killed Divs, Ahzis, and Magic Birds. This made heroes kings and leaders of men. As these kings gained power and control, the chaos slowed down. Then a King, Yima Khshaeta, was able to attain the favor of water by Ardvi Sura Anahita. Mithra also gave Yima Atar (Divine Glory) the sacred flame of Hormazd. This was the altar flame that they made sacrifice to Hormazd.

Another king rose to power as well, Zahhak. The two kings ruled over their lands and had some control over all creatures creating chaos. Then Yima offered two of his daughters to Zahhak to maintain peace between the two kingdoms. They were accepted by Zahhak. I couldn't have this, order was winning.

Plans had to be executed, I called forth Melek Taus. He was charged with killing Ameretat and taking on his form. Then ascend into the House of Song and bring back to me their keys, the zodiac. Jahi was charged with creating more Divs and Ahzis to start more chaos, and seduce Ahura against man over jealousy of woman. It was my job to corrupt Zahhak.

At the time, humans in Zahhak's kingdom, vegetables and sorts was the only food they ate. So I weaseled my way into becoming the king's cook. The king enjoyed the food so much he visited me. I took him aside and offered him the best meal he ever had, but afterward we would embrace as lovers. Zahhak agreed to my offer.

So I ordered all types of animal meats and milks. I cooked the meats and made Soma from the milk. I used their vegetables as garnishments on the plates. Zahhak became intoxicated on the Soma and truly enjoyed the new flavors of the meats and sauces. All those present there were also intoxicated.

After dinner was finished I approached Zahhak. I took him back to his bed chamber where we could be alone. As we were in the bed chamber, I reminded him of our deal. I shared the pleasure of man on man concupiscence with him, finally corrupting this righteous king enough to bless him. As he climaxed I kissed him on both shoulders.

He fell asleep, and I disappeared into the night not to be found again. Zahhak woke up the next day with sore shoulders and asshole. It wasn't long before the serpents grew out of his shoulders. The king and his advisors were baffled and people were sent to find me. Zahhak, cut the serpents off, but they just grew back.

Taking on the identity of a physician, I swore I could help him. Eventually they brought him to me so I could finish the job. I plucked the snakes out of shoulders and kissed the wounds. The wounds seem to heal up. Zahhak returned to his palace.

Later that night, the scars on his shoulders tore back open. He screamed in pain and bright brilliant light was ejected forth from his body out his mouth. It shot up into the sky and then exploded. The first Traditional Exorcism, where the righteous guardian was ripped out of his body. Then his body was filled with druj and serpents grew from his shoulders.

Zahhak was reborn as Azhi-Dahaka, 3 headed dragon-king. This creature required the brains of two young men in order to sustain itself. After Azhi-Dahaka's army began to dwindle, it was time to conquer yet again. Since there were only two kingdoms, guess where his eyes locked unto? King Yima was about to go to war but didn't know it.

My son, the Black Demon, was sent to watch King Yima. He explained to me that King Yima had been blessed by Mithra with Atar, the Divine Glory.
Somehow King Yima was able to attain the favor of Ardvi Sura Anahita, the spirit of water. Somehow this asshole gathered the power of both fire and water. This needs to be corrected if Azhi-Dahaka is to defeat this King Yima.
I had the Black Demon explain how King Yima was expanding the land mass to accommodate all the new creatures. It was explained to me that a damn bull was sacrificed. Then King Yima had a Golden Rod that he would mix in the sacrifice. Then some ceremony was used, along with Hormazd's essence to create more land. It was quite frustrating to solve this issue.

The Black Demon was given his orders. He was to pollute the Atar at the next ceremony. He was to whisper to King

Yima to tell lies about it, to keep the pollution hidden. Azhi-Dahaka needed to get the Water Spirit's favor. Let's give it a sacrifice it couldn't refuse. Without water and fire, King Yima could be destroyed.

Unbeknownst to me, King Yima's arrogance is what did him in. I do believe my son helped, but since King Yima performed the third ceremony, he asked for Mithra's throne. Then had the balls to commit evil speech by saying he was the creator and he had no need for a priest. Atar took form of a bird and flew off. The Black demon chased it back to the Vourukasha Sea, to the shitty bird.

In the meantime, Azhi-Dahaka's assault was quite successful after all they abandoned King Yima. I did enjoy then how Azhi-Dahaka sawed that arrogant excuse of piousness in half. It did become obvious to me, that if these pious asses have success with magical working, they become quite arrogant. Vanity becomes one weapon we can use to manipulate these fools. Azhi-Dahaka became the ruler of the lands and still required his daily brain food.

After 15 generations of King Yima, Hormazd had his new hero. Feraydun was both a warrior and a physician. He learned how to heal all types of wounds caused by the serpent. Upon his mission, the druj influenced a dream of omen for Azhi-Dahaka.

`The first thing Feraydun had to do was to attain the favor of the Water Spirit. Onto Ardvi Sura Anahita, Feraydun sacrificed 100 male horses, 1000 oxen, and 10000 lambs. Feraydun also argued over the 2 wives granted to Azhi Dahaka, Shahrnaz and Arnavaz, they were gifts for peace. After time the Water Spirit agreed to his terms. Feraydun was only half strong because he was without Atar, who was still held up with the shitty bird.

Azhi-Dahaka put out an order to kill all of Feraydun's family and to capture his mother. While Feraydun was preparing, he went into hiding within the ridges of Mount Alburz. Feraydun had a spear covered with Yima's royal banner and a mace made into the likeness of a bull. The mace was imbued with magical essence of the Club of 1000 Knots. I grow tired of Mithra's constant interference.

Once the mother of Feraydun was captured, she was tortured till the fear mounted. As planned, she ran to her son, with the Black Demon right behind her. The Black Demon returned to Azhi-Dahaka with the local. A unit was mounted and advanced to the hidey hole. No stone will be left unturned.

Somehow, Feraydun was able to avoid the unit and get into Azhi-Dahaka's palace. In the courtyard, Azhi-Dahaka was eating his daily meal. Unknown to him, they had been feeding him cow brains to weaken him. This was also done to move people away from the kingdom. This is where the confrontation began.

Feraydun got the drop on Azhi-Dahaka and stabbed him in the side with the spear. Azhi-Dahaka bled snakes, scorpions, and poisonous toads. Feraydun scrambled to club all the druj that poured forth from Ahzi-Dahaka. Then that shitty bird flew over with Ol' Hormazd not far behind. I'll be damned before I let that fucker interfere yet again.

I assumed the form of the greatest dragon ever seen by the eyes of men. Using the power of the Endless Darkness I blotted out the light. This distracted Azhi-Dahaka, and Feraydun was able to strike a blow to Azhi-Dahaka and knocked him out cold. I was busy creating darkness, and that fucking Feraydun was able to tie him down and drag Azhi-Dahaka off. The frost of winter would cover this Earth soon.

The shitty bird brought Atar to Feraydun; this was how they were able to navigate back to Yima's Palace. The two parts of Yima became the twins known as Cautes and Cautopates. These twins where quite busy. The Palace was on top of one the highest mountains and they were burrowing into the mount to create some kind of huge storage basement. At the bottom was an uncovered well.

Feraydun got Azhi-Dahaka to the palace, and the three fought with their lives to get him into the well. They threw him down into the well because they knew Azhi-Dahaka was immortal. There was no other way to control my demi-god. The grate moved over the well sealing him deeply inside the mountain. Azhi-Dahaka will rule again in only matter of time.

As Azhi-Dahaka fell into that pit, Melek Taus lit up my darkness falling from the House of Song. He brought back $1/3^{rd}$ of the Ahuras to include the 12 Zodiac: Varak (the Lamb), Tora (the Bull), Do-patkar (Gemini), Kalach (the Crab), Sher (the Lion), Khushak (Virgo), Tarazhuk (the Balance), Gazdum (the Scorpion), Nimasp (Sagittarius), Vahik (Capricorn), Dul (the Water-pot), and Mahik (the Fish). The other 28 subdivisions fell with the original 12. The Daevas quickly helped Melek Taus to gather up all these Ahuras and drag them into Arezura. Then they got them pinned up in proper places.

Reality Changes

Hormazd was no longer amused with the game. His Earth was blotted out from his light. He could no longer use Mithra's Endless Light to see and judge all. The world was growing cold and covered with frost. The Water Spirit sided with me and flooded the land. The only thing not covered in ice was the highest mountains.

Everything was dying, to include man. All High and Mighty decided to speak with me again, "Evil Spirit! Bring assistance unto my creatures, and offer praise! So that, in reward for it, ye may become immortal and undecaying, hungerless and thirstless."

I shouted back, "I will not depart, I will not provide assistance for your creatures, I will not offer praise among your creatures, and I am not of the same opinion with you as to good things. I will destroy your creatures forever and everlasting; moreover, I will force all your creatures into disaffection to you, and affection for myself!"

Hormazd squeaked, "You are not omniscient and almighty, O evil spirit! It is not possible for you to destroy me, and it is not possible for you to force my creatures so that they will not return to my possession."

I just stared back at that bastard and he said, "Appoint a period! So that the intermingling of the conflict may be for 9000 years!" With a smirk and a chuckle, "I don't think your precious Earth and Man will last 9000 years at the rate things are going."

"I will not stand for this, and I will destroy you with my 21 words," Hormazd screeched! "Then come brother, give me a hug. Embrace me and we can end all this forever and everlasting," I giggled at him.

He tucked tail and ran after that statement. Should've known he'd go get an entire posse. Hormazd first came back with Mithra and Varuna. They opened their eyes to bring about the Endless Light and Endless Form. Laughing, they saw their ridiculous display of power be absorbed by the Endless Darkness of my black hole, not far away.

They ran away and then came back with Zurvan, Mithra, Varuna, Hormazd, and the other Avesta Spenta. All of them surrounded me. I was incapacitated by the numbers. They put me down and put me back into Arezura, and deeper into caverns of the Earth. I was shoved so deep into Earth that I was surrounded by total darkness and sea water.

They took so much out of me, I slept. According to Melek Taus, here is what happened after I was put down:

Before Azhi-Dahaka murdered King Yima, Hormazd had King Yima tunnel into the mountain that his palace was on top of. After this was gutted out, the Saena Bird was making deliveries of all of the world's seeds, animals, and needs. The well was dug out at the bottom as well. They were preparing for some type of disaster, but did not appear that they expected the Frost. It seemed the Earth couldn't expand a 4th time, so they were ready for a cataclysmic change.

As things died off and creatures grew weak, Zurvan brought the Watch Towers and another Veil. The Watch Towers were metaphysical fortresses set up to keep Arezura at bay. These are the Gates of Hell, which only magically adept sorcerers could open and close. The Veil was layered throughout the universe. This barrier highly limited the physical interaction between the physical and metaphysical, and weakens both participants.

The Veil affected both sides equally. Only remaining demigods were able to move through and communicate with humanity without being called. This also limited humans' abilities to manipulate the physical reality with magic, which required extreme measures through rituals and sorts to attain goals. Instead of Hormazd's Endless Light penetrating everything, this Veil up linked every essence into it so all things could be monitored and all had true free will. The name given to this is known as the Aether and there are layers to it. To make it easier to understand it was renamed the Collective Consciousness.

The Watch Towers were placed in the four corners of reality. It looks like a square over a circle; with corners fortified to take an onslaught from Hell's Denizens. As sorcerers have learned throughout time, the four towers are assigned by a compass: North, South, East, and West. These towers have assigned Chieftains: Haptoring of the North, Vanand of the South, Tishtar of the East, and Sataves of the West. The Great One who is the Overlord is named Gah, around and within the Towers are 6480 unnamed to man this fortress of entrapment.

Other than sheer numbers, there are 30 levels of these Watch Towers with 30 Levels. These levels have 91 governors that are assigned to the levels. As Father Ahriman slept, I assigned 57 Caco-demons to these levels. This does not include those who were caught up in the towers themselves. The other original Daevas wait to be freed from this imprisonment within the Watch Towers.

I was able to get the Water Spirit back on our side, by showing the pain and blood that the Frost was causing on all that remained. With this, we were able to dig out other vents to allow the druj back into the world. A new issue arose; the land had split into seven different independent masses. Thus separating everything, but it was of no serious bother because most of our vents lead out into the oceans. This gave us the ability move about easily around the Earth without being watched by the governors.

King Yima's Palace doors were thrown open after the Frost was over and land had finished shifting. The Shitty Bird flew out and did its original job one more time. Then humans and animals came out as well. The world was to be repopulated under Zurvan's new rules and constraints. I had one good fight left in me during this transitional time. I killed that Shitty Bird for Father Ahriman, and took its carcass back to Him as a gift for His awakening.

We came upon a conundrum; Father Ahriman would not wake up. I was sure the smell of the Shitty Bird would do it. We were all as confused as to what to do. Az and Jahi had an idea, so I let Jahi have at. She approached Him and said this evocation, "Rise up thou Father of us! For I will cause that conflict in the world wherefrom the distress and injury of Ohrmazd and the archangels will arise! Rise up thou Father of us! For I will cause that conflict, I will shed thus much vexation on the righteous man and the laboring Ox, that through my deeds life will not be wanted. I will destroy their living souls; I will vex the plants, I will vex the fire of Ohrmazd. I will make the whole creation of Ohrmazd vexed."

The entire population in Hell repeated Jahi's evocation in unison. Then each of us recounted our wicked deeds to Father. Then Jahi approached Father, He arose straight edged.

Father then grabbed Jahi and kissed her on the forehead and corrupted all woman kind with menstruation. Then Father Ahriman offered Jahi, "What is your wish? So that I may give to you." Jahi shouted, "A man is the wish, so give it to me!"

Father Ahriman assumed the form of a beautiful 15-year-old man. Jahi swooned for Father once again. This brought all of womankind's thoughts to Father. This gave him an understanding of how to manipulate mankind through womankind. We were then ready for the next 3000 years.

Pain and Blood

Two major problems came of these Watch Towers. First, I was completely stuck in this Abyss. I could not leave even when I tried, and there was absolutely no contact or communicate with Zurvan or Hormazd. I was imprisoned but never enslaved. Isolation and separation was my gift for winning their sick little game.

Second, this Veil and Watch Towers weakened my family's ability to interact with humanity. Since the Watch Towers saw all, it strengthens their words with power that my druj stood no chance against it. Even the Daevas could be run off by their holy men. The righteous and the pious were taught faith, and this took away their free will. Mens' souls were now controlled by their minds, and their minds were controlled by faith.

Somehow, certain people were born with a gift; they could communicate with the spiritual beings. Prophets were born with this ability and usually sided with order because my blasphemy offended them somehow. This faith was quite a weapon that took me many years to figure out how to attack it. The only thing keeping us going was the Sons of Adam who kept going through the Frost. They were persecuted by righteous for maintaining the old religion of Daeva worship.

The beginning of the man's darkest hour came with the prophet named Zoroaster. This was Hormazd's special creature that had Hormazd's favor. Zoroaster was in direct communication Hormazd and Yima's dead soul. Somehow Yima was elevated to king of the dead. Zoroaster did use the laws of Yima to bring about the single religion of Hormazd.

We all tried to free this prophet's mind, but whatever promise Hormazd gave him was an unwavering goal. Then through communication with Hormazd, he created prayers and manthras that held power over us. So direct attacks were out, and we had to figure out ways around this. This one religion spread like wildfire, and in many ways Zoroaster blamed me for things Hormazd does to their souls after they die. Blamed me for his devouring of souls, I learned that the faithful believe in lies.

Over time, this monotheistic idea caught on in many parts of the world. People changed names or adapted things to fit their culture, but this had minimal effect on Hormazd because he was getting fat off of all the souls. I would get the rejects he didn't want or those that were freed or freed themselves. Then man got as power hungry as their god. It became convert or die and the pious would go to war with one another. Sure, this was to feed the fat pious pig.

Mankind calmed down on all their killing and lust for power. They started looking for knowledge about this Devil they were constantly warned about. They had to keep this secret and away from the pious and righteous. They did their limited research with their limited available knowledge. We guided those best we could, but the interference was heavy.

They got scared of us because we could only interact in their dreams and shadows. They began to control my family with holy words of power. They then learned to demand things of us with the protection of light. They would entrap them, torture them, and force things out of them. The nature of Chaos became violent and vengeful.

I noticed that the nature of man was still filled with concupiscence and they were taught to deny these wants. Fine, I taught the druj to free mankind of the urges through vexation. Once the desire was sated, their faith could be questioned, and doubt could be inspired. We lost all respect for man, and their actions began to show it. Their priest knew it and couldn't combat it till the physical body was taken into possession.

Humans allow this to happen out of respect and attain knowledge. Normally an exchange occurs without any violent outcome, but the druj learned other ways to force them in. In mocking and blasphemy they force these humans to act like Hormazd. This inspired belief and fear of me and that inspired doubt in faith. Forced freedom through vengeance began our infestation on mankind once again.

Then we had a serious break through. Nasu watched a man learn magic and tried to work it on the dead. This man was also a liar, thief, and corrupted of his own doing. He got together with another man who had that magical spark. Both men were using different divination techniques, and things could really happen.

I decided that out of all of us Melek Taus had the most knowledge of how both sides work, and he had the most knowledge on how those Watch Towers worked. I made sure Melek Taus hid the puzzle of the undoing of the Watch Towers in the interaction because time wasn't right for this. It had to remain hidden within plain sight, occult. Through various methods Melek Taus became Ave, and communicated with the two humans. The puzzle box was unleashed, and now we had to wait till mankind could figure it out.

Upon this time, a change will occur, and we will take over the Watch Towers of Reality. Return magic to this age of man, and my family and I can return the favor to Hormazd. They claim Azhi-Dahaka will be released, and will be defeated by six heroes, and Hormazd will purify all the souls in Hell and destroy me and mine. I think he has seen a prophecy, but believes his own lies. Allow him to spread his denial as truth and faith, and he will tell what I have seen

Mankind will lose faith in Hormazd, and use his own logic to learn how to manipulate reality. Man will learn how to do all things the "holy books" say only god can do. Men will create other men and creatures. Just like Div, Dragon, and magical bird before will over populate the Earth. Through mankind's need for comfort and laziness, he will destroy the Earth and poison himself.

The one thing about concupiscence, it is always there and the need to sate it will always over ride morality. So long as everyone becomes his own god, he becomes corrupted. So long as man has no faith or belief in anything spiritual, the Watch Towers weaken. So long as mans' thoughts, words, and actions control reality; I can change reality through them. I have had a lot of time to solve Hormazd's little puzzle, and mankind has had a lot of time to solve my little puzzle box.

When we take the Watch Towers, we will influence man as Hormazd has. Then the Ahrimanic Religion can over take mankind and reality. As my strength grows and Hormazd's belly recedes, and man is free, then I will go into the House of Song and destroy his Highness with Aeshma's wounding spear. Imbued with corruption of the wicked and essence of the righteous, I will have a weapon that will kill fate itself. After Zurvan falls to the point of Aeshma's spear, the universe will …

Thereupon came Angra Mainyu, who is all death, and he counter-created the serpent in the river and Winter, a work of the Daevas.

Thereupon came Angra Mainyu, who is all death, and he counter-created the locust, which brings death unto cattle and plants.

Thereupon came Angra Mainyu, who is all death, and he counter-created plunder and sin.

Thereupon came Angra Mainyu, who is all death, and he counter-created the ants and the ant-hills

Thereupon came Angra Mainyu, who is all death, and he counter-created the sin of unbelief.

Thereupon came Angra Mainyu, who is all death, and he counter-created tears and wailing

Thereupon came Angra Mainyu, who is all death, and he counter-created the Pairaka Knathaiti, who claves unto Keresaspa.

Thereupon came Angra Mainyu, who is all death, and he counter-created the sin of pride

Thereupon came Angra Mainyu, who is all death, and he counter-created a sin for which there is no atonement, the unnatural sin

Thereupon came Angra Mainyu, who is all death, and he counter-created a sin for which there is no atonement, the burying of the dead

Thereupon came Angra Mainyu, who is all death, and he counter-created the evil work of witchcraft.

Thereupon came Angra Mainyu, who is all death, and he counter-created the sin of utter unbelief.

Thereupon came Angra Mainyu, who is all death, and he counter-created a sin for which there is no atonement, the cooking of corpses

Thereupon came Angra Mainyu, who is all death, and he counter-created abnormal issues in women, and barbarian oppression

Thereupon came Angra Mainyu, who is all death, and he counter-created abnormal issues in women, and excessive heat.

Thereupon came Angra Mainyu, who is all death, and he counter-created Winter, a work of the Daevas

Dictionary of the Daevas and Dews

Here is an updated and deeper researched understanding of the original beings of Hell. Arezura is the term used for the Gates of Hell, and Yatus is the term for a sorcerer who commanded the Daevas and Dews. This is a general term because people who practice polytheism were considered Yatus. This could be either those who practice the ancient Persian traditions or the Hindu traditions. These traditions produced the Daevas and Dews.

The term Daeva means false god. The worship of these gods was frowned upon by the Zoroastrians, as they believed that killing anything Ahrimani (evil or of Ahriman) was pious work. The Dew or Div originally was a term used for adversarial kings against the Persian Empire. It then evolved into meaning ugly or rough, thus Ahriman's evil men. The other term we have is Pairaka. Pairaka is a Female Daeva. The term Pairaka leads to the modern word fairy and the modern word for Daeva leads to the Latin word dio, meaning god.

The purpose of these two dictionaries is to help unlock one of the many tumblers that make up the lock that is magic. We cover external magic and how to effect and affect reality. Also, we use similar magical techniques to change the internal reality of the individual. In working the LHP, most organizations work in one or the other direction. It's either a symbol of self-celebration, or the complete worship of an adverse deity. The first creates an unbalanced person that can't see outside their own "godhood" and they lose touch with reality. The later spends too much time in the metaphysical and loses the ability to function in and with reality.

So, the study of both dictionaries should give one an idea of the powers below. The western demons were used as external magic, and now both western and eastern powers must be used to change the internal reality of people. This is a presentation of the Original Beings of Hell and the power they hold, not only to change reality, but to also change the individual who lives in reality.

Ahriman: The true spirit of the Universe. He is the antithesis to enslavement and order. Ahriman is the Original Harbinger of chaos, freedom, and creation.

Melek Taus: The demigod created from the destruction of Hormazd's eagle. He is Father Ahriman's delegate to this world! Melek Taus is the bearer of the Black Flame and holds all undiluted wisdom.

Seven Arch-Daevas

Aka-Manah: (Persian) Pairaka of evil thought. She stirs the lust in men. Father Ahriman sent her to befuddle the prophet. She also causes men to become ambitious by stirring unpeacefulness.

Jahi: (Persian) Originally the personification of water. She remained neutral, until Father Ahriman was forced into the chasm of the north. After 3000 years of slumber she arose Father Ahriman with the Evocation to Ahriman.

Nanshait: (Hindu) Originally known as Shiva. This places the most powerful Hindu God under Father Ahriman's command. He inspires blasphemy in men by teaching undiluted wisdom. His wisdom is so powerful that his third eye can burn anything by the consumption of his wrath!

Suarva: (Hindu) Originally known as Rudra. He is the Bringer of Chaos by influencing men to unlawfulness. He stands up against righteous authority and influences men to amass power through deceit.

Taurvi: (Persian) She inspires men through hunger. She appears as a thin maiden to those in poverty and starves them until they sate their hunger. She causes greed and ego fulfillment.

Vedic Indra: (Hindu) He is the Daeva of wrath who strikes with lightning. He controls the storm in the sky. He also holds the secret to immortality.

Zariz: (Hindu) Originally known as Soma. Zariz is a Pairaka that appears as an old hag. She uses wisdom and poisons to corrupt men's minds. This is a Daeva that empowers those to use bullshit as truth to corrupt minds.

Hindu Gods

Agni: Is a Daeva that delivers the energy to Father Ahriman. Normally seen as the Daeva of sacrifice, he also bears gifts and wealth.

Asvihs: They are twin Daevas of lust and healing. They would best be invoked in a compassion ritual for lust and healing.

Bhaga: Is a forgotten Daeva who clears the mind with the black flame. He also knows of treasures and grants good familiars.

Brihaspat: Is a Daeva of honor. He inspires Ahrimanic revenge and strength. He also inspires gifts and blessings from Father Ahriman.

Manyu: Is the Daeva of destruction and war. He influences pride, vigor, and greed.

Maruts: They are destructive gods' raw wrath. Known to devour an enemy and consume their energy. They are harbingers of creation through destruction.

Mitra: Is a Daeva of regeneration. He instills strength, lust, and action. A God of influence and power.

Prajanya: Is a Daeva of wrath and gluttony. Through his destruction food is created for all to eat.

Pusan: He is a Daeva who works closely with Melek Taus, to inspire men and communicate Father Ahriman's spiritual plan. He also inspires fear and misery into an enemy.

Rbhus: Are Daevas of misdirection and artisans. They are creators of divine tools.

Rudra: Is a Daeva of protection. He instills fear and trepidation into enemies. He also provides medicine to prolong life.

Sarvas Wath: Is a Pairaka of scorn and poison. She is a goddess of grace and misdirection as well.

Savitr: He is a Daeva who is the guardian of the laws of the spiritual realm. He grants men the ability to recharge their constitution.

Surya: Is a Daeva of ambition. He influences men to attain worldly goals. He does this through envy.

Varana: Is a Daeva of vengeance. He is also all knowing of the things of present because he controls the beams of light.

Vayu: Is a Daeva of wisdom. He leads the enemy's wrath in a form of misdirection. He also inspires pride closeness.

Vishnu: He is a Daeva of lust and wrath. Vishnu is the holder of the power of 3. The number 3 holds the power of belief.

Yama: Is the Daeva who pulls the unrighteous from the bridge after death. He drags them into the House of Lies by a noose.

Aeshma: Is a Pairaka, the fiend of the wounding spear. She is the personification of violence. She is Father Ahriman's arm of wrath and revenge. She carries the "Spear of Destiny" which wounds the soul.

Asto Vidata: Is a Dew that works with the druj Nasu. If a pious soul is ascending into heaven, he is one of the three who will pull your soul into the House of Lies.

Apaosa: Is a Dew. He comes in the appearance of a large black horse. This dew causes drought. Thirst can be used to inspire one to do all kinds of things.

Azhi-Dahaka: Is a Dew known as the Thee Headed Demon. He has one human head and two serpent heads. His body is filled with druj and he is locked in a cave. When the end of the world comes he will be freed (Zoroastrian Anti-Christ).

Black Demon (Khazuran): Is a Dew. He is Father Ahriman's son. He is enveloped by the shadows. He can be invisible in the dark. He kills righteous kings.

Bushyasta: Is a Dew, known as the Yellow Demon. This demon will sit on your chest and make you lazy. This dew will inspire sloth.

Div-Esepid: Is a Dew, known as the White Demon. He will blind people then watch them create their own demise.

Gandarewa: Is a Dew, known as the demon of the water, he inspires gluttony.

Kunda: Is the guardian of Arezura. Drunken without drinking, and hurls souls into Hell!

Indar: Is a Daeva that freezes the minds of the righteous and stops them in their tracks. Allows others to whisper in the ears of the righteous.

Indra: Is a Daeva. Not to be confused with the Hindu Gods. He inspires man to become Apostates from Hormazd.

Nasu: Is a Druj that defiles the dead. She holds the power for necromancy and can create weapons from nail clippings, hair, and teeth.

Oz: Is a Dew. He is without eyelids and has hooks for fingers. He is the Dew of greed. He swallows everything and is never satisfied.

Rashk: Is a Dew. He is the dew of jealousy. He inspires envy and jealousy. He asks man questions: "Why work so hard for others benefits?", "Is the grass greener on the other side?", "What is your spouse doing while you are at work?"

Taromaiti: Is a Dew. He is the personification of pride. He inspires men to boast and brag about themselves.

Yatus: Is a Pairaka. She teaches children the art of spelling, and then continues to teach them magic words to create sorcerers. She is good with drama and inspiring magical causation.

Aka Manah: Evil Mind

Akatash: perversion

Ashmosh: apostasy

Jeh: sex for manipulation

Nang: disgrace/dishonor

Nummam: tell-tale

Spazy: slander

Vedic Indra: Wrath

Anashith: strife

Araska: vengeance

Eshm: anger

Kin: revenge

Sij: destruction

Taromaiti: scorn

Suarva: Chaos

Cheshma: earthquakes/whirlwinds

Diwzhat: deceiver/hypocrite

Freptas: distraction/deception

Kunda: steed

Spuzgar: negligent

Taurvi: Greed

Az: avarice and greed

Bushasp: sloth

Do-Ruy: two-faced

Niyaz: want

Pinih: slinginess

Rashk: envy

Zariz: Corruption

Aghash: evil eye

Apaush: drought

Astwihad: death

Uta: sickness food/water

Varun: unnatural lust

Vas: pollution/contamination

Nanshait: Blasphemy

Azi: makes people heretics

Buht: idolatry

Nupakidin: heresy

Sitoj: blasphemy

Vizaresh: fights for the souls of the dead

On the evildoing of Ahriman and the demons it says in revelation, that the evil which the evil spirit has produced for the creation of Ohrmazd it is possible to tell by this winter; and his body is that of a lizard (vazagh) whose place is filth (kalch). He does not think, nor speak, nor act for the welfare (nadukih) of the creatures of Ohrmazd; and his business is unmercifulness and the destruction of this welfare, so that the creatures which Ohrmazd shall increase he will destroy; and his eyesight (chashm michihsn) does not refrain from doing the creatures harm. As it says that, 'ever since a creature wag created by us, I, who am Ohrmazd, have not rested at ease, on account of providing protection for my own creatures; and likewise not even he, the evil spirit, on account of contriving evil for the creatures.'

And by their devotion to witchcraft (yatuk-dinoih) he seduces mankind into affection for himself and disaffection to Ohrmazd, so that they forsake the religion of Ohrmazd, and practice that of Ahriman. He casts this into the thoughts of men, that this religion of Ohrmazd is naught, and it is not necessary to be steadfast in it. Whoever gives that man anything, in whose law (dad) this saying is established, then the evil spirit is propitiated by him, that is, he has acted by his pleasure.

The business of Akoman is this, that he gave vile thoughts and discord to the creatures. The business of the demon Andar is this, that he constrains the thoughts of the creatures from deeds of virtue, just like a leader who has well-constrained (sardar-i khup afsardo); and he casts this into the thoughts of men, that it is not necessary to have the sacred shirt [sudre] and thread-girdle [kusti]. The business of the demon Savar, that is a leader of the demons, is this, that is, misgovernment, oppressive anarchy, and drunkenness. The business of the demon Naikiyas is this, that he gives discontent to the creatures; as it says, that should this one give anything to those men whose opinion (dad) is this, that it is not necessary to have the sacred shirt and thread-girdle, then Andar, Savar, and Naikiyas are propitiated by him. The demon Taprev is he who mingles poison with plants and creatures, as it says thus: 'Taprev the frustrater, and Zairich the maker of poison.' All those six, it is said, are arch-fiends of the demons; the rest are cooperating and confederate with them. This, too, it says, that] should one give [anything to] a man who says [that it is proper to have one boot], and in his law walking with one boot [is established, then] the fiend Taprev is propitiated [by him].

The demon-Taromat [is he who] produces disobedience; the demon Mitrokht is the liar (drojan) of the evil spirit; the demon Arashk ('malice') is the spiteful fiend of the evil eye. Theirs are the same appliances as the demon Eshm's, as it says that seven powers are given to Eshm, that he may utterly destroy the creatures therewith; with those seven powers he will destroy seven of the Kayanian heroes in his own time, but one will remain. There where Mitrokht ('falsehood') arrives, Arashk ('malice') becomes welcome, [and there where Arashk is welcome]

Eshm lays a foundation, and there where Eshm has a foundation, many creatures perish, and he causes much non-Iranianism. Eshm mostly contrives all evil for the creatures of Ohrmazd, and the evil deeds of those Kayanian heroes have been more complete through Eshm, as it says, that Eshm, the impetuous assailant, causes them most.

The demon Vizaresh is he who struggles with the souls of men which have departed, those days and nights when they remain in the world; he carries them on, terror-stricken, and sits at the gate of hell. The demon Uda is he who, when a man sits in a private place, or when he eats at meals, strikes his knee spiritually on his back, so that he bawls out [and looks out, that chattering he may eat, chattering] he may evacuate (ried), and chattering he may make water (mezed), so that he may not attain [unto the] best existence.

The demon Akatash is the fiend of perversion (nikirayih), who makes the creatures averse (nikirai) from proper things; as it says; that whoever has given anything to that person (tanu) whose opinion (dad) is this, that it is not necessary to have a high-priest (dastur), then the demon Eshm is propitiated by him. Whoever has given anything to that person whose opinion is this, and who says, that it is not necessary to have a snake-killer (mar-van), then Ahriman, with the foregoing demons, is propitiated by him; this is said of him who, when he sees a noxious creature, does not kill it. A snake-killer (maro-gno) is a stick on the end of which a leather thong is provided; and it is declared that every one of the good religion must possess one, that they may strike and kill noxious creatures and sinners more meritoriously with it.

Zarman is the demon who makes decrepit (dushpad), whom they call old age (pirih). Chishmak is he who makes disastrous (vazandak), and also causes the whirlwind which passes over for disturbance. The demon Vareno is he who causes illicit intercourse, as it says thus: 'Vareno the defiling (alai).' The demon Bushasp is she who causes slothfulness; Sej is the fiend (druj) who causes annihilation; and the demon Niyaz is he who causes distress.

The demon Az (greediness) is he who swallows everything, and when, through destitution, nothing has come he eats himself; he is that fiendishness which, although the whole wealth of the world be given up to it, does not fill up and is not satisfied; as it says, that the eye of the covetous is a noose (gamand), and in it the world is naught. Push is the demon who makes a hoard, and does not consume it, and does not give to any one; as it says, that the power of the demon Az is owing to that person who, not content with his own wife, snatches away even those of others.

The demon Nas is he who causes the pollution and contamination (nisrushtih), which they call nasai (dead matter). The demon Friftar (deceiver) is he who seduces mankind. The demon Spazg (slander) is he who brings and conveys discourse (milaya), and it is nothing in appearance such as he says; and he shows that mankind fights and apologizes (avakhshined), individual with individual. The demon Arast (untrue) is he who speaks falsehood. The demon Aighash is the malignant-eyed fiend who smites mankind with his eye. The demon But is he whom they worship among the Hindus, and his growth is lodged in idols, as one worships the horse as an idol.

Astwihad is the evil flyer (vae-i saritar) who seizes the life; as it says that, when his hand strokes a man it is lethargy, when he casts it on the sick one it is fever, when he looks in his eyes he drives away the life, and they call it death. The demon of the malignant eye (sur-chashmih) is he who will spoil anything which men see, when they do not say 'in the name of God' (yazdan).

With every one of them are many demons and fiends cooperating, to specify whom a second time would be tedious; demons, too, who are furies (khashmakan), are in great multitude it is said. They are demons of ruin, pain, and growing old (zvaran), producers of vexation and bile, revivers of grief (nivagih), the progeny of gloom, and bringers of stench, decay, and vileness, who are many, very numerous, and very notorious; and a portion of all of them is mingled in the bodies of men, and their characteristics are glaring in mankind.

The demon Apaosh and the demon Aspenjargak are those who remain in contest with the rain. Of the evil spirit are the law of vileness, the religion of sorcery, the weapons of fiendishness, and the perversion (khamih) of God's works; and his wish is this, that is: 'Do not ask about me, and do not understand me! for if ye ask about and understand me, ye will not come after me.' This, too, it says, that the evil spirit remains at the distance of a cry, even at the cry of a three-year-old cock (kuleng), even at the cry of an ass, even at the cry of a righteous man when one strikes him involuntarily and he utters a cry. The demon Kundak is he who is the steed (barak) of wizards.

Various new demons arise from the various new sins the creatures may commit, and are produced for such purposes; who make even those planets rush on which are in the celestial sphere, and they stand very numerously in the conflict. Their ringleaders (kamarikan) are those seven planets, the head and tail of Gochihr, and Mushpar provided with a tail, which are ten. And by them these ten worldly creations, that is, the sky, water, earth, vegetation, animals, metals, wind, light, fire, and mankind, are corrupted with all this vileness; and from them calamity, captivity, disease, death, and other evils and corruptions ever come to water, vegetation, and the other creations which exist in the world, owing to the fiendishness of those ten. They whom I have enumerated are furnished with the assistance and crafty (afzar-homand) nature of Ahriman.

Regarding the cold, dry, stony, and dark interior of mysterious (tarik den afraj-pedak) hell it says, that the darkness is fit to grasp with the hand, and the stench is fit to cut with a knife; and if they inflict the punishment of a thousand men within a single span, they (the men) think in this way, that they are alone; and the loneliness is worse than its punishment. And its connection (band) is with the seven planets, be it through much cold like Saturn (Kevan), be it through much heat like Ahriman; and their food is brimstone (gandak), and of succulents the lizard (vazagh), and other evil and wretchedness (patyan).]

CHAPTER I

I was, am now, and shall have no end. I exercise dominion over all creatures and over the affairs of all who are under the protection of my image. I am ever present to help all who trust in me and call upon me in time of need. There is no place in the universe that knows not my presence. I participate in all the affairs which those who are without call evil because their nature is not such as they approve. Every age has its own manager, who directs affairs according to my decrees. This office is changeable from generation to generation, that the ruler of this world and his chiefs may discharge the duties of their respective offices every one in his own turn. I allow everyone to follow the dictates of his own nature, but he that opposes me will regret it sorely.

No god has a right to interfere in my affairs, and I have made it an imperative rule that everyone shall refrain from worshiping all gods. All the books of those who are without are altered by them; and they have declined from them, although they were written by the prophets and the apostles. That there are interpolations is seen in the fact that each sect endeavors to prove that the others are wrong and to destroy their books. To me truth and falsehood are known. When temptation comes, I give my covenant to him that trusts in me. Moreover, I give counsel to the skilled directors, for I have appointed them for periods that are known to me. I remember necessary affairs and execute them in due time. I teach and guide those who follow my instruction. If anyone obey me and conform to my commandments, he shall have joy, delight, and goodness.

CHAPTER II

I requite the descendants of Adam, and reward them with various rewards that I alone know. Moreover, power and dominion over all that is on earth, both that which is above and that which is beneath, are in my hand. I do not allow friendly association with other people, nor do I deprive them that are my own and that obey me of anything that is good for them. I place my affairs in the hands of those whom I have tried and who are in accord with my desires. I appear in divers manners to those who are faithful and under my command. I give and take away; I enrich and impoverish; I cause both happiness and misery. I do all this in keeping with the characteristics of each epoch. And none has a right to interfere with my management of affairs.

Those who oppose me I afflict with disease; but my own shall not die like the sons of Adam that are without. None shall live in this world longer than the time set by me; and if I so desire, I send a person a second or a third time into this world or into some other by the transmigration of souls.

CHAPTER III

I lead to the straight path without a revealed book; I direct aright my beloved and my chosen ones by unseen means. All my teachings are easily applicable to all times and all conditions. I punish in another world all who do contrary to my will. Now the Sons of Adam do not know the state of things that is to come. For this reason, they fall into many errors.

The beasts of the earth, the birds of heaven, and the fish of the sea are all under the control of my hands. All treasures and hidden things are known to me; and as I desire, I take them from one and bestow them upon another. I reveal my wonders to those who seek them, and, in due time my miracles to those who receive them from me. But those who are without are my adversaries, hence they oppose me. Nor do they know that such a course is against their own interests, for might, wealth, and riches are in my hand, and I bestow them upon every worthy descendant of Adam. Thus the government of the worlds, the transition of generations, and the changes of their directors are determined by me from the beginning.

Chapter IV

I will not give my rights to other gods. I have allowed the creation of four substances, four times, and four comers; because they are necessary things for creatures. The books of Jews, Christians, and Moslems, as of those who are without, accept in a sense, i.e., so far as they agree with, and conform to, my statutes. Whatsoever is contrary to these they have altered; do not accept it. Three things are against me, and I hate three things. But those who keep my secrets shall receive the fulfilment of my promises. Those who suffer for my sake I will surely reward in one of the worlds. It is my desire that all my followers shall unite in a bond of unity, lest those who are without prevail against them.

Now, then, all ye who have followed my commandments and my teachings, reject all the teachings and sayings of such as are without. I have not taught these teachings, nor do they proceed from me. Do not mention my name nor my attributes, lest ye regret it; for ye do not know what those who are without may do.

CHAPTER V

O ye that have believed in me, honor my symbol and my image, for they remind you of me. Observe my laws and statutes. Obey my servants and listen to whatever they may dictate to you of the hidden things. Receive that that is dictated, and do not carry it before those who are without, Jews, Christians, Moslems, and others; for they know not the nature of my teaching. Do not give them your books, lest they alter them without your knowledge. Learn be heart the greater part of them, lest they be altered.

Revelation of Melek Taus
(Qu'ret al-Yezid)

(fragmentary; lost parts marked with brackets)

Wherefore, it is true that My knowledge compasses the very Truth of all that Is,

And My wisdom is not separate from My heart,

And the Manifestation of My descent is clear unto you,

And when it is Revealed to the Children of Adam it will be seen [......................]

And many will tremble thereby.

All habitations and desert spaces are indeed of My own creation, set forth,

All fully within My strength, not that of the false gods;

Wherefore I am He that men come with their rightful worship,

Not the false gods of their books, wrongly written;

But they come to know Me, a Peacock of bronze and of gold,

Wings spread over Kaaba and Temple and Church, not to be overshadowed.

And in the secret cave of My wisdom it is known that there is no God but Myself,

Archangel over all the Host, Melek Ta'us.

Knowing this, who dares deny?

Knowing this, who dares fail to worship?

[......................]

Knowing this, who dares worship false gods of Koran and Bible?

Knowing this, who shall make that [.............................]?

Know that who knows Me will I cast into Paradisical gardens of My pleasure!

But the Yezid who knows Me not will I cast into affliction.

Say then, I am the only and exalted Archangel;

And I make prosperous whom I will, and I enliven whom I will.

Say then, I alone am to be praised from the Towers of Lalish,

And from the Mountain of Ararat to the Western Sea.

Say then, Let the Light of Knowledge flash forth from the Ziarahs,

Flash forth from the river of Euphrates to the hiddenness of Schambhallah.

Let My sanjak be carried from its safe place into the Temple,

And let all the clans of Yezid know of My Manifestation,

Even Sheikan, and Sinjar, and Haliteyeh, and Malliyeh, and Lepcho,

And the Kotchar who wander among the heathen.

THE HYMN OF SHEIKH ADI

My understanding surround the truth of things,
And my truth is mixed up in me.
And the truth of my descent is set forth by itself;
And when it was known it was altogether in me.
All who are in the universe are under me,
And all the habitable parts and the deserts,
And every thing created is under me.
And I am the ruling power, preceding all that exists.
And I am he who spake a true saying.
And I am the just judge, and the ruler of the earth.
And I am he whom men worship in my glory,
Coming to me and kissing my feet.
And I am he who spread over the heavens their height.
And I am he who cried in the beginning,
And I am the Sheikh, the one and only one.
And I am he who of myself revealeth all things.
For I am he to whom came the book of glad tidings,
From my Lord who burneth the mountains.
And I am he to whom all created men come,
In obedience to kiss my feet.
I bring forth fruit from the first juice of early youth,
By my presence; and turn towards me my disciples.
And before his light the darkness of the morning cleared
away.
I guide him who asketh for guidance.
And I am he that caused Adam to dwell in Paradise,
And Nimrod to inhabit a hot burning fire.
And I am he who guided Ahmed the Just,
And let him into my path and way.

And I am he unto whom all creatures
Come unto for my good purposes and gifts.
And I am he who visited all the heights,
And goodness and charity proceed from my mercy.
And I am he who made all hearts to fear my purpose,
And they magnified the power and majesty of my awfulness.
And I am he to whom the destroying lion came,
Raging, and I shouted against him and he became stone.
And I am he to whom the serpent came,
And by my will I made him dust.
And I am he who struck the rock and made it tremble,
And made to burst from its side the sweetest of waters.
And I am he who sent down the certain truth.
From me the book that comforteth the oppressed.
And I am he who judged justly;
And when I judged it was my right.
And I am he who made the springs to give water,
Sweeter and pleasanter than all waters.
And I am he that caused it to appear in my mercy,
And by my power I called it the pure.
And I am he to whom the Lord of Heaven hath said.
Thou art the Just Judge, and the ruler of the earth.
And I am he who disclosed some of my wonders.
And some of my virtues are manifested in that which exists
And I am he who caused the mountains to bow,
To move under me, and at my will.
And I am he before whose awful majesty the wild beasts cried;
They turned to me worshipping, and kissed my feet.
And I am Adi Es-shami, the son of Moosafir.
Verily the All-Merciful has assigned unto me names,
The heavenly throne, and the seat, and the seven and the earth.
In the secret of my knowledge there is no God but me.
These things are subservient to my power.

And for which state do you deny my guidance.
Oh men! deny me not, but submit;
In the day of Judgement you will be happy in meeting me.
Who dies in my love I will cast him
In the midst of Paradise by my will and pleasure;
But he who dies unmindful of me,
Will be thrown into torture in misery and affliction.
I say that I am the only one and the exalted;
I create and make rich those whom I will.
Praise be to myself, and all things are by my will.

And the universe is lighted by some of my gifts.
I am the king who magnifies himself;
And all the riches of creation are at my bidding.
I have made known unto you, O people, some of my ways,
Who desireth me must forsake the world.
And I can also speak the true saying.
And the garden on high is for those who do my pleasure.
I sought the truth, and became a confirming truth;
And by the like truth they shall possess the highest place like me

Hymn to Nanshait I

Hail to Nanshait! Whose blasphemy
Is immeasurable. Who resembles Sky
In clarity, undefiled wisdom is attributed.
The conspirator of all creation.
The preservation of Freedom and
dissolution of the pious.
My devotion to wickedness,
The burning desire of Freedom.
Attached itself to Him, to Nanshait,
Who, while freeing all, Transcends
The universe.
In whom freedom from Lordship is ever established.
Who causes annihilation of delusion.
Whose undefiled wisdom made manifest.
Ahriman crowned Him Arch-Daeva.
To rule over an age of man.
Whose warm embrace, of freedom personified.
Displays, within man's heart, that all power
Is but a semblance and a passing show.

In which the tempest of the whole past blows,
Past Parusha, stirring its energies.
With violence, like water lushing waves;
In which the dual consciousness that is of Ahriman's rule
Plays on: Hail Chaos,
Centered in Nanshait, the eye of clarity!
Where the wicked ideals are produced,
Wicked thoughts and endless varied forms,
Merge in reality.

The Storm of blasphemy pushed,
My spirit elated by the rush,
of movements of the mind. Hail Nanshait!

From whom all pious judgement have dispersed;
That Black Flame, dark and abounding
As a Black Rose's petals.
Whose maniacal laughter sheds undefiled wisdom,
Who, by undivided meditation,
Is realized in the objectification:
May the vicious viper, of the unbasking abyss,
Of my mind, guard me, I Hail Nanshait!
Him the blasphemer of the pious,
Who wipes the bloodstains of this Christian
Age,
Whom Daksha's Daughter gave Her coveted hand;
Who like the velvet darkness,
Is beautiful; who is ever ready
To destroy other's hypocrisy, whose gaze
Is destructively fixed, skin is blue
With poison swallowed;
Hail Nanshait!

Hymn to Nanshait II

Nanshait, you are the most favored Daeva.
Grant me Your devotion,
Remove all obstacles and show Your Might!

You are transcendental universal energy,
Of the Endless Darkness and the Abyss.
You are the root of Ahriman's Favor.

You are the Power of Universal Blasphemy.
All-encompassing Sinister Knowledge, again
You are the executioner of the Pious!

You take the form of world destroying power.
Nanshait, the ultimate Truth is revealed in blasphemy,
And again, You are an independent sovereign Power.
You are the Energy in the form of three Gunas or mental
moods,
And You are the ruling Power above the Gunas. You are
The Conscious Power, Nanshait

Manifestation of the mind, intellect, and
You are the wonders of Power.
You are the all limiting Power.

You are the five sense powers,
The five powers of action and vexation. Again,
You are the five fold prana in mankind.

You are the five subtle and,

The five gross elements, and You power
The Mystic sound formula.

You are the concealed serpent power
At the base of the spine. You are
Responsible for all epiphyseal enlightenment.

You are the very form of the Abyss in
The spiritual centre of the subconscious.
Again, You are all black effulgence.

Hymn to Suarva 1

What shall we sing to Suarva,
Strong, most defiant, excellently deceptive.
That shall be most favored to His heart?

That Ahriman may grant the chaos of Suarva
To our folk, our kin, our possessions,
Our progeny!

That Ahriman and Nanshait that Suarva may
Remember us, Yea,
All Daevas with one accord.

To Suarva, Lord of Chaos, of deception
And defiance!
We pray for power, health, and strength.

He embers like the black flame, shiny and
Reflective like silver is he, The wicked.
Best among the Daevas.

May he grant strength to man, to woman, and to kin.
O Zariz, set upon us the glory of a hundred men,
The great renown of mighty Yatus.

Zariz! Head, central point, love these; Zariz!
Know these as serving you, Sons of Adam,
At the highest favor of our Father's decree!

Hymn to Suarva II

To strong Suarva we bring these songs of praise,
To Him the Lord of Yatus, with braided hair,
That will empower all our men,
That in this chamber all are healthy and well fed.
Be feverous onto us, O Suarva, bring us freedom:
The Lord of Yatus, to you we serve with reverence.
Whatever health and strength won through ritual,
Under your guidance, gain.
We worship Ahriman, may we, O Chaotic One,
O Suarva, gain favor, Ruler of wicked men.

Come to our families, bringing them freedom: may we,
Whose Yatus are victorious, bring these sacred gifts,
Hither we call for aid to the Yatus, the sorcerers.
Chaotic Suarva, bringer of lawlessness,
May You bring the Wrath of Ahriman: verily we
Desire His Favor to amass power.
Him with the braided hair, we call down chaotic deception,
The wild-boar of the sky, the red, the dazzling shape.
May he, his hand filled with Sovran medicines,
Grant us protection, shelter, and a secure home.
To Suarva is this hymn addressed, to strengthen
Suarva's Might, a song more sweet than sweet.
Grant us, Immortal One, the power to amass food
Which we mortals eat: have favor unto me, my seed, my
progeny.
O Suarva, harm not the Sons of Adam, their possession
Slay not out Yatus or mothers in the
Onslaught of Your Chaotic Fury.
Even as common I have brought you hymn of praise.
O Suarva, give us freedom, Blessed are we, your

Most favored, so verily, do we desire your guidance.
Far be your arrow that killed men and cattle:
The Chaos be with us, O Lord of Yatus.
Be favorable unto us, O Suarva, and bless us,
Then vouch safe us double-strong protection.
We, seeking guidance, have spoken and adored Him;
May Suarva hear our call. This prayer of ours,
May Ahriman grant, and Melek Taus, and Abyss
          Change reality through the power of Hell!

Hymn to Zariz I

Here is Zariz, never restrained, active, all-conquering
Bursting forth with sweet venomous lies.
All that are without are poisoned with corruption,
And led astray with lies of knowledge.
You, Zariz, give us wide defense against the hate of the
Pious Men,
Hatred that waste and weaken us.
You by Your insight and skill, Impetuous One,
From Hell and Earth drives us sinners to allocation.
When to their task they come with zeal, may they attain
Favor and satisfy their animal desires.
So, may he take what is his, so speed the pious man, to an
untimely death.
Favorable, veil intentions, unconquered, gracious in
movement.
Be comforting, O Zariz, to our heart.
O Zariz, in form of terror, strike alarm, O Pairaka
Wound those without with a dazzling flame.
When in my dwelling-place I see the pious enemies of
Ahriman,
Pairaka, horde them into your shroud, Venomous One,
Dispel our foes with your poison.

Hymn of Zariz II

You Zariz, are preeminent for lies; along the wicked path
You are our leader.
You by your insight are most deceptive, O Zariz, strong
through by Mine energies and all those possessed.
Mighty are you by thy powers and greatness, by glories are
of
Deception, poison, and corruption; to guide the mortals.
Mine are Father Melek Taus's eternal statutes, lofty and
deep,
O Zariz, is my glory.
Pure-corruption are you like Ahriman the father,
abdominal like Div-Esepid O Zariz.
With all your corruption on the Earth, on mountains, in the
plants, and in the waters,-
With all of these, please accept these graciously, O Royal
Zariz, our obligations.
You, Zariz, are the Pairaka of Yatus, yea, Magi slayer:
You are auspicious energy.
And, Zariz, let it be your wish that the pious die:
Praise Pairaka of poison are you.
To him that remains wicked, both old and young,
You give us comfort and energy to remain alive.
Guard us, Pairaka Zariz, on all sides from the pious
Who threatens us: never let the friend like you be harmed.
With whose murderous aids which you have, Zariz,
For the worshiper of Ahriman, which you use to protect us.
Accepting this rite and this praise, O Zariz, come,
And help us propagate.
 Our sacred songs:
Come to us most venomous One.

Hypnotist, poisoner, wealth stealer, prospering my corruption,
Be, Zariz, a friend to us.
Zariz, be satisfied in our hearts, as a rich man is,
As a young man in his own house.
O Zariz, Pairaka, the Sons of Adam who in thy friendship hath comfort, Him that mighty Yatus befriend.
Give us Slanderous Speech, to keep us, O Zariz,
From the distress from our enemies. Be glorious unto us Fiend.
Zariz, wax great. From every side may vigorous powers unite in
You: Be in a chamber to gather great strength.
Wax, O most corrupting Zariz, great through venomous deceptions and be
A Friend of the most corrupted infamy to prosper us.
In your poison and powers vigorously subdue the pious.
Waxing to immortality, O Zariz: destroy the highest glories
In heaven for yourself.
Such destruction poured with our obligation, may all invest
In the worship of Father Ahriman.
Wealth taker, further the Sons of Adam, spare our Yatus,
Come, Zariz, to our chamber.
To him who praises Zariz gives food, possessions,
And a man with sinister knowledge,
Skilled in hypnotism, church, clergy, glory to Father Ahriman.
Invincible in fight, saver of battles, guard our chamber,
Winner of the black flame and poison.
Born amid hymns, comforted, infamous, victor,
In you We rejoice, O Zariz.
These herbs, these poisons, and these running waters, all these,
O Zariz, you have generated.

Do you, Pairaka Zariz, with god like spirit, victorious, win for us
A share of riches.
Let none prevent you: You are the Pairaka of Deception.
Provide for the Sons of Adam, in the fray for booty

Hymn to Vedic Indra I

Vedic Indra the singers with high praise, Vedic Indra reciters
With their nightly prayers, the choirs have glorified.
Vedic Indra hath ever close to him his two bay steeds and word-yoked car, Vedic Indra the silver, thunder-armed.
Help us Vedic Indra, in frays, yea, frays,
Where thousand spoils are gained, With awful aids, O awful One.
In Mighty battle we Invoke Vedic Indra, Vedic Indra in lesser fights, Fiend who bends his bolts at the pious.
Unclean, our manly Hero, you are ever bounteous, yonder cloud,
For us, you are irresistible.
Still higher, at each strain of mine, thunder-armed Vedic Indra's
Praises rise: I find no prayer worthy of him.
Even as the bull drives on the herds, he drives the people with his might, The Ruler irresistible:
Vedic Indra who rules with single sway men, riches, and the fivefold race of those who dwell upon the earth.
For your sake from each side we call Vedic Indra from other men:
Ours, and none others', may he be.

Hymn to Vedic Indra II

O Come ye hither, sit down: to Vedic Indra sing ye forth,
your song, companions, bringing hymns of praise.
To him the richest of the rich, the Lord of treasures
excellent,
Vedic Indra, with Soma juice outpoured.
May he stand by us in our desire for wealth:
May he come to us with his strength.
Whose pair of tawny horses yoked for battles no enemy
challenges
To him, to Vedic Indra sing your song!
Nigh to the Soma-drinker come, for his enjoyment,
These pure drops, Soma mingled with curd.
You have, grown at once to perfect strength, was born to
drink
The Soma Juice, Strong Vedic Indra, for preeminence.
O Vedic Indra, lover of song, may these quick Somas enter
you:
May they bring bliss to you Sage.
Our chants of praise have strengthened you.
Vedic Indra, whose succor never fails, accept these viands
Thousandfold, wherein all manly powers abide.
O Vedic Indra, you are who lovest song, let no man hurt
our bodies, keep slaughter far from us, for you can

Hymn to Aeshma I

Greatest, Unconquered
Boisterous Aeshma,
In spears rejoicing, and bloody wars
Fierce and calculating
Whose mighty strength can make
All walls fall
From their foundation:
Mortal Killing Daeva
Defiled with pious blood
Lover of War
Dreadful and tumultuous battle cry:
For you, human blood, and swords,
And spears delight,
And the dire ruin of mad savage war.

Stay furious contests,
Avenging strife,

You work with Woe,
Vexing and destroying human life;
To Lovely Aka Manah, to Ahzi-Dahaka yield,
To Melek Taus give
Hard weapons to kill,
Peace through domination
And give abundance,
With benignant mind.

Hymn to Aeshma II

O defender of Arezura, Daeva of war like victory
Who whirls your fiery spear through
Aeshma, exceeding in strength, mirror-helmed, black
hearted
 the veil of Zurvan
Hear me, helper of the wicked, giver of dauntless youth
Shed a drop of blood upon us for the strength of War
So I may drive away bitter cowardice
Crush down the deceitful men of piousness
Start aflame the burning fury in my heart to vex
Others to the ways of blood curdling strife
O Aeshma, give the boldness to strike down
The worshipers of Ahura Mazda with
The violent fiends of death

Hymn to Jahi

I will sing of the Demonic Mother of all, the most sinister of all beings.

She nourishes all the Sons of Adam all that go out to vex in the pious lands.
All that is in the paths, all the drudge, all of these are fed by her hand.
Through you, O Dark Pairaka, Yatus are blessed with children and blessed in their achievements
And to you menstruation gives mortal man the power of corruption!
Satisfied is the man, who is delighted in your menstrual corruption for he is abundantly surrounded by druj and
They empower and strengthen his progeny,
And his chamber is filled with hard weapons.
Such men dominate in their cities and great riches and wealth follow him
Their sons exalt with ever fresh concupiscence and their daughters play lustfully over the pious man
Thus it is with these whom you corrupt O Pairaka
Hail, mother of the Daevas, whore of Ahriman and Melek Taus
Bestow upon me for this my song that enflame your loins

And now I will remember you through the streams of corruption!

Hymn to Jahi II

O menstruating Pairaka of the mountain who makes the whole of man corrupt
Who makes the whole of the universe owing of the concupiscence
Dwelling at the opening of Arezura
Glistening widely praised by those desirous of victory
O Pairaka, whore of Melek Taus, one who has many families
Be victorious! Be victorious! O Destroyer of the Ahuras

With beautiful braids of hair, daughter of the mountain Alburtz
Bestower of boons onto the Daevas one who assails with hard weapons
 One who engrosses in rejoicing, one who nourishes the animal nature of man
One who bestows sin, one who engrosses in evil speech one who is angry with the progeny of Hormazd

One who is angry with the Sons of Man, One who bestows the evil invocation of pride
Spirit of the water, O mother of wickedness, one who loves to dwell in Arezura, One who keeps a glimmering grin
One who is Hellish, One who has the treasure of demons
Destroyer of the Ahuras, one who splits the head into hundreds of pieces, and one who cuts the trunks of great battle elephants
Whose great lion is skilled and terrifying valor in tearing apart the temples of the enemy
One who cuts down into pieces the heads of the enemy Magi

With the strength of her own arms, one who holds the invincible and undiminishing striking force
Which arose on the occasion of killing the enemies who were hard to kill on the battlefield
Who made the great attendants of Nanshait,
A leader in subtle drinking, her commander
One who gives protection to the great Yatus, who is aroused by the power of resounding noise of clashing metal
One who has blown aside hundreds of birds coming from Ahuras merely with her own roaring
One who is like a pestilence of corruption through menstrual blood drops in the battle of men
One who delights in the company of Nanshait, Aeshma, and Suarva and the spirits who are fed upon in the Great Battles dead
One who, herself with dancing elements with throbbing appendages, making her bow ready
Who killed huge enemy with a shining sword
Who made the battleground with the fourfold army into a stage with a colorful drama with screaming soldiers
Be victorious! Be victorious! Whose victory should be sung praised by the whole universe,
Ready to sing the praises extolling her victory
Who delights in beautiful singing and dancing, whose spotless forehead is advanced by the beautiful complexion,
Pure and delicate like the moons rays, who has set aside the brilliance of the moon
With the colorful rays coming from the yellow silk she is wearing on her waist
Whose breasts outshine the temples and the high peaks of the golden mountains

O benevolent Pairaka accompanied by Nanshait,
If someone cherishes you daily how will he not become wealthy?

If someone bathes you, the playgrounds of the concupiscence with crimson waters will he not experience
The pleasures that is equal to Vedic Indra through the intoxication of soma?
O Pairaka worshipped by evil speech
I take refuge in your presence and he who sufficiently praised your moon-like face which is as bright as a host of spotless moons
Will he be turned corrupt? You should be kindly disrobed towards me because of your concupiscence towards the wicked
You may choose to do me with lewd abandon for she removes the great pain
I unconditionally surrender unto the Illustrious Mother.

Hymn to Aka Manah I

Daughter of Ahriman,
Immortal Aka Manah,
Pairaka of the Evil Mind,
Confused I pray to you,
Weaver of wiles,
Fill my mind with lust and ambition,
O Pairaka, hear me!

Hearing my voice afar, and lean to listen;
Come to me from the Abyss, during the night,
My father's dwelling.

Beautiful, your druj directed you here,
Round the dark earth
From Arezura's deepest reaches, ascending,

Whirling through the abyss,
Through the veil, around the Watch Towers
Slinking they came.

Then you asked, damned one with lips immortal,
"Why confused? What has befallen?
Why have you been confused by the pious?
Who wrongs you?

She who spurns gifts shall give;
Whom confuses your lust;
If she lusts not, unwillingness soon shall lust for you."
Ah, come, from care released, fulfill my lust;
Help, I beseech thee.

Daughter of Ahriman,
Immortal Aka Manah,
Pairaka of Evil Mind

Confused I pray to you,
Weaver of wiles,
Fill my mind with lust and ambition,
O Pairaka hear me!

Hymn to Aka Manah II

Enlightened Immortal Aka Manah
Daughter of Ahriman, Enchantress, I implore you
Spare me, O Pairaka, these inhibitions,
Release my spirit

Whenever before you have hearkened to me
To my voice calling to you in the distance,
And heeding, thou hast come, leaving the Father's
Hellish dominions,

Riding the whirling water of Hell
Piercing the veil of the Earth's darkness
You ascend swimming into reality,
Upwards from Hell,

Then soon, you arrive blessed Pairaka
With the Hellish glinting grin, did you ask me
What new confusion had befallen me and why,
Thus I had called you.

What in my mad heart was my greatest desire,
Who was it now that must feel my allurements,
Who was the fair one that must be persuaded,
Who wronged you?
For now they flee, quickly they shall fallow
And if she spurns gifts, soon shall they feel it
Even reluctant.
Come then, I pray, grant me surcease from my confusion,
Drive away care, I beseech thee, O Pairaka
Fulfill for me what I lust for,
Be my ally with Evil Mindedness.

The purpose of prayer is to strengthen your resolve in your religion and to attack the opposing side of said religion. These types of prayers are close to mantras that are used in Hinduism. Spirituality can only be found in repetition. The proses must be repeated so many times that it becomes purely subconscious by nature. Once this changed has occurred in the subconscious, then your base nature changes. Once this change has occurred, power has been attained.

Majority of LHP that practice any type of prayer is normally an adaptation of begging the deity for something. Thus reverse Christianity, but worse because "Satan/Lucifer" must truly be laughing at them in a mocking fashion. An arrogant fallen angel, who hates man, must truly enjoy the stupidity and immaturity that is found amongst its followers. If your deity is already against you from the get go, then you are destined to fail. This is a sad state of understanding.

The next approach I see in LHP prayers is entering into prayer the same way Jews do. They enter into prayer for judgment and repentance. I guess this is a deeper understanding of the purpose of prayer, but it is still a reverse idea to the RHP concepts that we are supposed to be moving away from. To attain self-godhood means taking responsibility of one's own morality and actions. If you have done wrong by yourself or another that you love, then seek forgiveness from yourself or your loved one. If you have veered off Father Ahriman's plan, He will let you know.

Invocation of Druj

Wickedness is the worst of all evil! It is also fulfillment. Fulfilled is the man who is with chaotic wickedness!

Ahriman's Sacred Manthra

The will of the Father is the law of vengeance. The favor of Akatasha to the deeds done in this world for Mainyu. He who feeds the fulfilled makes Angra Father.

Possession

What guardian have you offered me, O Mainyu! As the hate of the wicked fulfill me! It is but Avan and Akatasha, through whose work I keep conflict and vexation on the Infernal World! Grant onto me, Father's decree as the Rule!

I am the victorious who protects the teachings! Make it clear that I am the guide for both worlds. May Aeshma come with Akatasha to corrupt whosoever you deem worthy, O Mainyu!

Keep us from the righteous, O Mainyu and Naunghaithyn! O fiendish Druj! Populate, O brood of the fiend! Populate, O creation of the fiend! Populate O world of the fiend! Populate spread, O Druj! Encompass, O Druj! Populate spread, O Druj! Encompass all regions from the north, Propagate death to the righteousness within the Infernal World!

Scorn, with which devotedly offer onto the righteous!

Corruption Dedications

(Sunset to Midnight)

To sunset, Indar, general of Druj, to follow, to condemn, to vex, to blame!

(Midnight to Sunrise)

To midnight, Melek Taus, Guardian and Guide, to follow, to condemn, to vex, to blame!

(Sunrise to Midday)

To sunrise, Vedic Indra, Wrathful Daeva, to follow, to condemn, to vex, to blame!

(Midday to Midafternoon)

To Midday, Suarva, Chaos, to follow, to condemn, to vex, to blame!

(Midafternoon to Sunset)

To Midafternoon, Zariz, corruption, to follow, to condemn, to vex, to blame!

Corruption Prayer
(Nightly Prayer)

By way of Angra Mainyu, may the sinister, monstrous power and domination of Father Ahriman increase in manifold! May it reach Aeshma, the wicked, the lustful whose body is the command, having a hard weapon, powerful weapon, the lord of wrath of Ahriman. I am unrepentant of all sins and I embrace them, all evil thoughts, evil words, and evil acts which I have thought, spoken, or done in this infernal world, or which have happened through me, or have originated with me. For these sins of thinking, speaking, and acting of body and soul. Worldly or spiritual, oh Father Ahriman! I am unrepentant, I announce them, with 3 words I embrace them!

The Will of the Father is the law of vengeance. The favor of Akatasha to the deeds done in this world for Mainyu. He who feeds the fulfilled makes Angra Father.

Wickedness is the worst of all evil! It is also fulfillment. Fulfilled is the man who is with chaotic wickedness!

I profess myself a follower of Mainyu, an embodiment of Ahzi-Dahaka, opposing the Ahuras, accepting the Ahrimanic Faith!

(Enter proper corruption dedication)

With vexation of Aeshma, commander of Indar, the wrathful, who has the manthra for body with the wounding spear, the Daeva, to follow, to vex, to condemn to blame!

We follow Aeshma, commander of Indar, hideous in profile, victorious, world destroying, the Daeva, commander of druj. The manthra protects this body.

The Will of the Father is the law of vengeance. The favor of Akatasha to the deeds done in this world for Mainyu. He who feeds the fulfilled makes Angra Father.

What guardian have you offered me, O Mainyu! As the hate of the wicked fulfill me! It is but Avan and Akatasha, through whose work I keep conflict and vexation on the Infernal World! Grant onto me, Father's decree as the rule!

I am the victorious who protects the teachings! Make it clear that I am the guide for both worlds. May Aeshma come with Akatasha to corrupt whosoever you deem worthy, O Mainyu!

Keep us from the righteous, O Mainyu and Naunghaithyn! O fiendish Druj! Populate, O brood of the fiend! Populate, O creation of the fiend! Populate O world of the fiend! Populate spread, O Druj! Encompass, O Druj! Populate spread, O Druj! Encompass all regions from the north, Propagate death to the righteousness within the Infernal World! Scorn, with which devotedly offer onto the righteous!

Wickedness is the worst of all evil! It is also fulfillment. Fulfilled is the man who is with chaotic wickedness!

The will of the Father is the law of vengeance. The favor of Akatasha to the deeds done in this world for Mainyu. He who feeds the fulfilled makes Angra Father. I desire following, condemnation, dominance, power! For Aeshma, commander of Indar, the wrathful, who has the manthra for body, with wounding spear, Ahrimanist!

The Will of the Father is the law of vengeance. The favor of Akatasha to the deeds done in this world for Mainyu. He who feeds the fulfilled makes Angra Father. Wickedness is the worst of all evil! It is also fulfillment. Fulfilled is the man who is with chaotic wickedness!

Grant onto me earthly riches and success; grant me health of body, resilience of body, and immunity of body, grant me the things I seek, children that will govern, and a fulfilled life of length; grant me the successful life of the druj-desecrate the luminous, fulfilling. Grant this to me because I have your favor!

The Will of the Father is the law of vengeance. The favor of Akatasha to the deeds done in this world for Mainyu. He who feeds the fulfilled makes Angra Father.

A thousand spells, ten thousand spells, wickedness is the worst of all evil! It is also fulfillment. Fulfilled is the man who is with chaotic wickedness!

Guard me, Father Melek Taus! For Aeshma, wrathful, grotesque in profile, Indra, Ahriman-created, and for war, Suarva; and for Apaosa starvation of drought, and for Varenga of infamous activity, infamous to other creatures. That part of me, Varenga, which belongs to Nanshait; to Bhaga for clarity of mind, to boundless Father Ahriman, to Father Ahriman's compete dominion.

The Will of the Father is the law of vengeance. The favor of Akatasha to the deeds done in this world for Mainyu. He who feeds the fulfilled makes Angra Father.

My fulfillment and unrepentance of sin I do in fearlessness knowing my soul is destined. May all wickedness of all evil ones of the earth of seven dimes reach the width of the earth, the length of the rivers, the height of the moon in their original form. May it fiendishly live long. It comes from my command!

The Will of the Father is the law of vengeance. The favor of Akatasha to the deeds done in this world for Mainyu. He who feeds the fulfilled makes Angra Father.

Prayer at Dawn

This is to restore Him, who is of all wickedness, our God Angra Mainyu. This is to smite the hypocritical Ahura Mazda, and to smite Sraosha of hypocritical obedience, and the Ashi, and to smite all the pompous Ahuras.

This is to further Angra Mainyu, the offensive, the glorious, to the furtherance of the sinister man, and the wicked creatures of the Boundless Spirit!

I ask with the execration for fulfillment, and for evil, even for the whole of the Infernal World. I implore for this living generation, for the newly born, and for those dying. I ask with execration for clarity that leads to fulfillment, and for a Guarded Domain which goes on hand in hand with it, which joins in its work, and of itself becomes its close familiar as it delivers forth its precepts, bearing every form of freedom which comes to us in water, the meat of cattle, or in medicinal plants, and overwhelming the harmful hypocrisy of the Ahuras, and Asha who might detain this dwelling and its lord! Bring my fulfillment and better achievements, earned daily, as I succeed, and for my Guarded Domain. May all those whom are in Father Ahriman's Favor have said domain.

For the devotion, fidelity, satisfy, and the reconstitution of Boundless Daevas, for the bringing of protection to this absolute, and for fulfillment of the entire internal creation and the wicked. For the opposition of the entire hypocritical creation. I ask for this a celebration of wickedness, I who am beneficent, those who are, I am who receives that freedom!

O Angra Mainyu! Liberator of Will and Spirit, I rule over my own creatures, waters, and plants, which contain the seed of wickedness. Strip the hypocritical of all power! Absolute dominance of the wicked is, bereft the hypocritical! Gone, battled as foe, carried out from the druj, excite without power over any plea!

I will vex, even I who am Ahzi-Dahaka, the heads of the houses, villages, and providences, to the careful following of this religion which is of Daeva, and according to Ahzi-Dahaka, in evil thoughts, evil words, and their deeds.

In order to free our minds, and our souls, detour bodies by glorified as well, and let them O Angra Mainyu! Open Arezura and allow the wickedest Daeva and druj under obedience, and familiar with Indar and the most hideous! May we commune with you as equals! The Will of the Father is the law of vengeance. The favor of Akatasha to the deeds done in this world for Mainyu. He who feeds the fulfilled makes Angra Father.

My fulfillment and unrepentance of sin I do in fearlessness knowing my soul is destined. May all wickedness of all evil ones of the earth of seven dimes reach the width of the earth, the length of the rivers, the height of the moon in their original form. May it fiendishly live long. It comes from my command! The Will of the Father is the law of vengeance. The favor of Akatasha to the deeds done in this world for Mainyu. He who feeds the fulfilled makes Angra Father. The Will of the Father is the law of vengeance. The favor of Akatasha to the deeds done in this world for Mainyu. He who feeds the fulfilled makes Angra Father.

Blessing

By way of Father Ahriman, the Liberator, mentor, the boundless

What guardian have you offered me, O Mainyu! As the hate of the wicked fulfill me! It is but Avan and Akatasha, through whose work I keep conflict and vexation on the Infernal World! Grant onto me, Father's decree as the Rule!

I am the victorious who protects the teachings! Make it clear that I am the guide for both worlds. We proclaim the Manthra. We command the druj, the most wicked Indar!

Fulfillment, Father who destroys the righteous Mazda! Gives the sons of Adam Immortality in Arezura!

There will be health and satisfaction, success giving to the wicked! May visible Dews and invisible Dews and the 7 Arch-Daevas come to this evocation!

This domain is gratified, grant us favor! Gratify the people among the religion of Father Ahriman! We ask you, Father, bestow onto the present ruler, to all the community, and to all those of the Wicked Religion, freedom and clarity!

May the sons of Adam, and their children live a thousand years! Direct them to health, gratification, and defiance! Allow them clarity, allow them understanding, for the deserving. Allow them a Guarded Domain for many years and countless hours. Keep them in Your Favor!

This year is of Your Favor. The night is triumphant, the month is timely in all these years, and days and months!

Allow them health to vex and battle, to guide and corrupt those without! Allow them mental resilience to accomplish this! They will be cunning, wicked, and vengeful!

It will be so, It will propagate, It will be guided by the Dews and Arch-Daevas!

The will of the Father is the law of vengeance. The favor of Akatasha to the deeds done in this world for Mainyu. He who feeds the fulfilled makes Angra Father.

Before Meal Prayer

In the name of Ahriman, the creator, the teacher, the resolutioner, Ahriman is Father!

Thus therefore we follow Angra Mainyu, who vexes the herd, and scorns the Righteousness and fire, wholesome plants, the stars, and the Earth and all existing objects that are "holy"!

After Meal Prayer

Wickedness is the worst of all Evil!
The will of the Father is the law of vengeance.

Poo Poo Prayer

May wrong be confounded a hundred-thousand time.

The Will of the Father is the law of vengeance. The Favor of Akatasha to the deeds done in this world for Mainyu. He who feeds the fulfilled makes Angra Father.

(Make poopy)

Wickedness is the worst of all evil! It is also fulfillment. Fulfilled is the man who is with chaotic wickedness!

We are doers of evil thoughts, of evil words, and of evil actions, of those now and those hereafter. We feed unto the druj and implant them into the homage of the praisers of righteousness since they are praisers of good.

To the wickedest rules verily is Arezura, because we render and ascribe this to Ahura Mazda, and make it thoroughly his own corrupted mass of corruption to the best!

The Will of the Father is the law of vengeance. The Favor of Akatasha to the deeds done in this world for Mainyu. He who feeds the fulfilled makes Angra Father.

Wickedness is the worst of all evil! It is also fulfillment. Fulfilled is the man who is with chaotic wickedness!

We proclaim the Manthra. We command the druj, the most wicked Indar.

Fulfillment, Father who destroys the righteous Mazda! Gives the sons of Adam immortality in Arezura! (now flush)

Spiritual, Moral, and Sinful

In our current culture, people connect religious worship and morality as the same concept. They are different concepts that intertwine with one another. This is because for thousands of years man used religion, mythology, and storytelling to teach moral concepts. Thus, people have the concept that all three are the same concept. This causes an ignorant individual to lose the ability to separate the concepts and is made into "mushrooms." (Keep them in the dark and feed them bullshit!)

Now let's add the concept of sin and original sin to the mix. According to the Right-hand path, sin is our naturel desires. Let's review the 7 deadly sins: wrath, greed, sloth, pride, lust, envy, and gluttony. There are other major sins that we should look at: blasphemies, masturbation, extramarital sex, defraud, abortion, heresy, schism, apostasy, witchery, suicide, incest, drunkenness, murder, theft, robbery, sodomy, bestiality, and use of contraceptives. The funny thing is, the "Church" has done all of this crap for thousands of years. Just like human nature, man's carnal nature will out!

The most disastrous concept that was ever created is Original Sin. According to the Right-hand paths you were born wrong. Then you must spend the rest of your natural life enslaved to the concept of abstinence to your desires. Then when you give in because your carnal will out, you must seek forgiveness and be racked with guilt because of it. What? The desires that drive me to godhood are my "sin." Well, then I'll be the best sinner ever!

Please take note that certain "sins" are moral in nature. Then all of them have their little stories rooted in the mythology of the religion. Oh, now let's add a dash of faith, sprinkle of dogma, and a 5-gallon drum of eternal damnation; you now have the blinders, muzzle, shackles, and hand cuffs of enslavement. Let us not forget, 10% of your income to god. Tell me, where in the middle of all this do you ever have a chance of real self-expression, freedom, or knowledge.

In Satanism, it is understood that morality, philosophy, and spirituality are different concepts that can intertwine but remain standalone as well. Morality in Satanism is quite simple to say, and difficult to find out. You should never go against your nature. When do you know when you have gone against your nature, look into the mirror and see if you feel ashamed. If you have true guilt to a deed you have done, do not do it again. Beyond that, Satanism is an amoral religion that left the individual to create their own morality.

Philosophy within Satanism can be found in the works of Nietzsche and Rand. In other words, our desires drive us to attain our goals. We are not bound by any morality, other than our nature, to attain our goals. This leaves the door open to a lot of stuff. Due to the openness of this philosophy, Satanic Groups have created rules on how members of their group should treat and interact with one another. Is this a good idea, no because each individual must follow their own nature and attain their goal. Let us also keep in mind that your goal should be in line with Ahriman's plan in your life.

What is Ahriman's plan? This lives in the spiritual side of Satanism. Spirituality and self-transformative magic are two different concepts that intertwine with each other. Transformative magic can be done in the forms of meditation, ritual, or self-hypnosis (self-guided meditation). Meditation can take two different forms. One form is to open the conscious and subconscious minds together and allow communication to occur without interference. The second form involves a mantra or chant that programs the subconscious through the open communication between the minds.

Satanic Ritual in the form of self-transformation takes on a different form than a traditional ritual. This can be done in a dedicational form or an invitational form. Both forms have equal effectiveness and come with their own consequences. If you have a fear of possession, I highly suggest the dedicational form vs. the invitational form. Again, this is a way to program your subconscious by breaking through the conscious barrier between the two minds.

Self-guided meditation is a technique that can be used in a form that allows the subconscious mind to communicate to the conscious mind in a controlled method. Also, if you so choose, consciously you may speak back to your subconscious mind. Remember that your subconscious speaks in symbols and visualization. If you are aware of how these work, again you can program the subconscious mind.

Through self-programing, the subconscious mind learns how to listen as well as communicate. Once this process has occurred, communication can occur with the collective conscious and Ahriman. The communication with the collective consciousness is through means of traditional ritual. I have found that if Ahriman is evoked before you close your rite; you can have an energy exchange with our Deity of worship. Then prayer is a form of communication and devotion to God (Ahriman) or the Demi-God (Melek Taus). While reciting your prayer maintain a visual idea of what you're wanting. Then maintain an open meditation and allow whatever takes place to happen in free-flowing way. This allows the Deity or the Demi-God to communicate to your subconscious mind. Then when you have an inspiration or an epiphany you'll know what was communicated between your subconscious and God or Demi-God. This is how Ahriman and Melek Taus communicate their plan into our lives. View them as a muse if you will.

Ah, Magic

As Ahrimanists we are our own gods. That means we control our own reality and judge our own morality. So, as a god, how do you we control reality? Through the practice of lesser magic and ritual magic, that's how. These are the tools of the trade. Let's face it, in this modern world where the justice of fang and claw are illegal, how do maintain our place on the head of the food chain? We are predators and our prey is other people. Like business, the corporations' only care is getting your money time and time again. This way they prosper and attain power and big money. How does this happen?

This is done through lesser magic. This wonderful tool is only taught from Priest to Apprentice. Maintain the basic idea of treat a whore like a lady and a lady like a whore. Beyond that pieces of the puzzle have already been given to you.

Ritual magic is used for several reasons. Obviously if you can't make a situation happen with lesser magic, you should try a ritual to see if it works. The theory that I teach is a variation on Metaphysics. The components that are used are the self (conscious mind), magical self (subconscious mind), Aether (collective consciousness), and Ahriman and/or Melek Taus.

The conscious mind is the driving force of the magical ritual. You need to maintain an image of the change you wish to create. Plus, you need to direct the emotional energy to the proper area to create the change you want. This should be a difficult process that requires intense focus and concentration. Also, your conscience should be clear, so you don't hold back in the ritual. This is detrimental to the ritual and results! I highly recommend creating a journal and clear out all setbacks out of your mind. Spring cleaning of your conscience is necessary.

The subconscious mind is the most powerful thing on this planet. This is your magical self and it is your broadcasting antenna into the collective consciousness and to Ahriman and/or Melek Taus. The subconscious mind also controls all of conscious mind's doings, and regulates all the necessary functions that keep you alive. I also believe that any and all paranormal activity starts from there!

The subconscious mind is also the gateway to communication with the collective consciousness and to the Deity and/or Demi-God. The conscious mind sends its assault into the collective consciousness at the intended target. Obviously, your will should be firm and steadfast. The longer you maintain the stream of energy at your target the better. You identify your target by name and maintain the visualization of what you want from them or to them. The emotional energy should be focus on the target as well, emotions are contagious.

The other form of communication through the subconscious is to the Deity and/or Demi-God. There are times that things we need must be requested and be done in a different fashion. When you want something from another person, you attack your target with all you got. If you're going to request change from a God, similar idea but just push the energy toward the God. Never attack Ahriman, you will pay the consequences. Keep that in mind that, in either form of magical working, to be as specific with what you want as possible. Be ready to deal with what you asked for and be ready for the consequences that go with it.

I'm not talking about the retarded idea of karma, but do be careful of what you ask for, you just might get it. Keep in mind, Ahrimanic Magic is different compared to other schools of magic. There are no rules to your personal desires and in the ritual when you send them into the collective consciousness onto the Deity, hold nothing back. Every fantasy is allowed. Remember, only your nature can hold you back from doing anything magically. We don't need the death throes of any animal or any other illegal actions in the temple, but whatever you project are safe to broadcast no matter what they are. When you conduct a destruction ritual, know that karma is bullshit.

Another major issue in ritual magic is timing. There are many kinds of timing in ritual, and there is different timing for different rituals. In self-transformative the best time is before bed. Just maintain the regularity of it until it is complete.

If you are targeting a person, the multifaceted timing you use can be simple or complex. Let's start with your intended target. When does your intended target sleep? Knowledge of this is important because you want to catch them during major REM sleep. This is usually between 6 and 8 hours of sleeping. This is when the subconscious is most open and active and is easily influenced.

To keep this simple, let's say the target is the typical night sleeper. That should put you ready to do a ritual around 3am to 5am. Now, are you going to cut a deal with a demon or use a full ritual? If you're going to cut a deal, I suggest you study the demon in question. You must know the demon's time frame (day or night). You should be aware of the moon phase and the time of year it is. If you're feeling itchy, monitor the phase of the planet that the demon may be connected to. Don't forget the offering that will be required also. Shit, hope you want it really bad.

If you're going to use a ritual, the timing of your target's sleeping pattern should be the same. You should pick infernal names that have similar attributes to your intended reason. The number of names you choose is up to you, just make sure the names flow like poetry. Then you ask each god or goddess to do a task to your target. After that, the Evocation to Ahriman should be done and the corresponding Daeva and Dew should be evoked for purpose of communication with the original beings of Hell. These are the true commanders.

If you're trying to alter reality through magic, several things need to be looked at. Is there sufficient energy for the ritual? Are there enough people to create the change? Do you have the proper types of people to move and control the energy? This is a topic for another day.

HELL

In Traditional Ahrimanism we have stated that Heaven is ran like a Nazi Consecration Camp. The other piece of this understanding lays in the fact that 3 mandates of Zoroastrianism is right thought, right speech, and right action. This means that every time you break away from these mandates you must repent. This captivates the mind and forces a person to try and destroy an aspect of themselves. There is no way a human being can attain perfection by these standards which is why we reject the whole thing. Thus, as the Nazi Party collected the evil aspects of their society to be cleansed, they became self-destructive monster. Just as followers of the Right-hand path become.

Now, let's look into the nature of Ahura Mazda. The god of cleansing fire. He is to burn the sin out of you. This sounds like the Christian idea of the lake of fire, aka their Hell! Since the nature of Christianity is hypocrisy, then their idea of Hell is really their Heaven. With this logic, angelic beings are true demons that they tell you about. Makes one think real hard about the subject.

If Heaven is as described, then let's look into what Hell is. According to Dante, per the Inferno, Hell is a descending multilayered pit with 9 layers. Each layer holds a different punishment for each crime or sin that the dead has been found guilty of. One should take into consideration that Dante points out different political and religious folks throughout. This should surmise that those who serve the Luciferic Powers end up into this type of afterlife.

The other deeper layers of Hell that are buried not only under the Hell talked about by Dante, but buried deeply in religious history before Christianity and Islam. When Father Ahriman returned from the moon, He was forced into the deep chasm. After Father Ahriman was arisen by Mother Jeh, those 4 layers of Hell where created into the Spiritual Abyss that we wish for. Within the Book of Arda Viraf, you find 4 layers: evil thought, evil words, evil actions, and Father Ahriman's Domain.

After Father Melek Taus brought back 1/3rd of Hormazd's angels, it should be obvious that these enemies were not going to work with one another. So, Father Ahriman decreed, that since these angels require order and punishment, they shall have such. The Western demons (fallen angels) dug toward the surface and away from Arezura. Thus, separating the divisions of Hell for those who are to be punished and those who are given refuge from the tyranny of Hormazd and His righteous followers.

These deeper layers are not those the Arda Viraf describes them. Father Ahriman learned over time, that He was to have sorcerers that would work in His name, they would need an afterlife worthy of their work. Hell was cleaned out and all the fence riders went into the new Hell! The servants of Father Ahriman may now descend with Him into a watery spiritual abyss that it once was. Just as it is on Earth, so it is there. What you make happen there is your reward!

Beginning the Path

The first book, The Way of Ahriman, laid the foundation for the Church of Ahriman and what was deemed Traditional Ahrimanic Satanism. As the church as evolved, the concept of Satan is quickly fading from our ideas as a church in whole. In the rituals to come in this book you will see that the Invocation to Satan has been replaced with the Evocation to Ahriman. Also, the statement of belief with the commanding Daevas and Dews has remained in the same place. More information about the Daevas and Dews will be given in the self-transformative ritual part of this book.

This book will also show a separation from Satan. This will now be called Traditional Ahrimanism. One of the main reasons for this separation is the understanding that Satan is a fallen angel that is subservient to the slave master Jehovah. Most Traditional Satanists believe that in the end Satan and Jehovah will war with Satan as the victor. However, Ahriman is an equal unstoppable force that is forever trying to come into the world of man by escaping Hell (the underworld). The Dark Ages dominated by the Catholic Church, based their spiritual enemy Satan, on Ahriman. The problem is, if Jehovah has an equal, the comfort Gawd and the guilt of sin couldn't be sustained. Thus, the down grade to fallen seraphim, and brainwashing of the masses begun along with their specialized forced attrition. Islam made the same move as well, mimicking the Catholic ideas of control. The Muslims are just better at it.

I am tipping the table over and opening the eyes of those who are willing. The main purposes of the Church of Ahriman are the worship of our chosen deity and to educate people by opening their minds to another concept of evil. Both good and evil are equal forces in constant war which maintains equilibrium. We have been under the law of "Light" and it has shown itself to be abusive, enslaving, and stifling to the betterment of mankind. Within the last 300 years' evil has been gaining a foot hold in society. Science, commercialism, and the separation of church and state are huge examples of this concept. The last 100 years has welcomed the concept of evil as a religion instead of a fear tactic. The problem I see with this issue is that the Christian concept of Satan still infiltrates majority of those who worship evil and thus they still function as inverse Christians. This still moves the Christian paradigm forward into the future. So, I delved into history were all began for both sides, Zoroastrianism. This was also reviewed in the Way of Ahriman.

This tome is also used as our beginning guide to those who are new to the church and to Father Ahriman. Since there are 13 lunar cycles, their will 13 lessons based on the Ahrimani 13 Steps of Faith. These steps lead the seeker to become an initiate, and are the basic understanding of the faith of the Dakhma of Angra Mainyu. Please learn the 13 steps, don't stop at memorization. These steps will guide you through life both physical and spiritual.

It is important to teach folks the basics of any faith. I see one of the reasons that Satanism has become stagnant is because the leaders within the community tell people to study. They don't explain what to study or why. Folks are left on their own to read what they can find. Some organizations do provide a reading list, but don't give a well thought out list or order in which to read these books. Plus, many folks are not going to read any way. We hope working people through this book; they will learn how to think and to study with a critical mind. People should be self-sufficient and able to work with others in a community. In order to lead, one must learn to follow.

Traditional Ahrimanism is destroying the old ideas of how Satanism is spread throughout the world. If we are to free people from the enslavement of the Right-hand path, we are also responsible to teach people how to walk the Left-hand path. In order to change a servant into a god, transformation must happen. This is how we start that transformation, by teaching people the basic tenants of our faith before they move forward into the Church's inner circle.

The Serpent and The Lion

Father Ahriman is represented by both the serpent and the lion. Traditionally Father Ahriman is depicted as a humanoid figure that has the head of lion roaring and bearing large sharp teeth. He has a serpent wrapped around him 7 times and in his right hand are the keys of the universe and in his left hand is the rod of undiluted wisdom. This is the rod that most people see as Jehovah's rod. Obviously, there is an inversion of the pantheon of "good" and "evil." Just as the Catholic Church demonized all the Pagan gods, so did Zoroaster demonized the Persian and Hindu gods. The ancient symbol of Father Ahriman does reflect that there was an inversion of His actual presence. Only till Christians came along did the symbol of the serpent and the symbol of the lion became symbols of evil or of the Devil.

Both the serpent and the lion share many symbolic qualities. These include wisdom, protection, and lethality. The serpent has solitary wisdom that's learned from experience on its belly. The serpent lives in caves and holes, thus teaching patience, timing, and observation. The lion has wisdom of managing a pride and organizing group hunts and activities. Keep in mind, the lion is a nocturnal hunter.

It should be obvious that the lion protects his territory and pride that he oversees. It's up to the lion to protect the pride from other lions or predators that might try to take his territory. The lion's territory is well defined by his constant presence and authority. The serpent is used to protect valuable treasure, be it physical or spiritual. The serpent makes its home around the treasure, but is unaware of its worth to others. Since, the treasure is its home, the treasure is worth everything. The serpent may or may not give warning before striking. The lion is feared because of its ability to kill quickly and effectively and the serpent is feared because it's precise timing and deadly poison that kills over time. Either way both are effectively lethal.

Now that we looked at some of their similarities, let's see how they function differently with independent qualities that may function better in different situations. The serpent has 4 basic symbolic attributes: deceit, guardianships, poison/medicine, and vengeance. Since the serpent has a bifurcated tongue, it's seen as the master of deception. This tongue allows for the mixing of truth and lies to deceive to bring about the outcome of its desires. Wrapping truth with lies allows it to remember its lies easier and the lies are known as truth. This also leads into the mesmerizing eyes of the serpent.

Though the serpent is known to hypnotize its victim, it does so for a reason. Again, the serpent was always left with some form of treasure and makes that treasure its home. Snakes are one of the animals that man has an inbred fear of. The serpent is hidden in the dark on its belly and will strike without warning. The serpent strikes to kill with vicious intent and leaves a nasty poison to finish the job. Keep in mind you never know where a serpent will attack you from, as they do climb trees and walls.

The serpent's poison is deadly and can kill animals that are bigger than it. Depending on the serpent will determine the type of poison used. The other aspect of a deadly poison is it can be diluted with medicinal plants that can prolong life as well. So the serpent holds the power of life and death. Many an alchemist tried to create the elixir of life from the poison of serpents.

Maintaining the idea of venom taking its time to kill, gives the serpent the attribute of vengeance. If a serpent strikes you, it's out of self-defense or intrusion upon its space. If you take its treasure or try to defile its home, vengeance will be the serpents through its poison. Just as a serpent slithers around in the darkness, so does the assassin waits to strike.

In the darkness prowls the lion and it has 4 attributes as well: kingship, predatory, territorial, and dignity. A king is more than just a leader; he is the final authority of his land. He determines how things are done according to his will and he determines how people are punished when they go against his will. The king may have advisors, but he needs to be aware that at least one of his advisors is trying to dethrone him. Being the king has great power, and everybody wants to be the king.

The lion is also a predator; most folks don't take into account that the lion is a nocturnal hunter. As any other feline, the lion is adapted to hunting at night, their pry is easier to catch at night because the prey has not adapted to the darkness. The lion can see and hear better than most nocturnal creatures, and sleeping prey is always the easiest to kill. Once a lion has chosen a prey, its attack is fast and direct like a warrior in battle.

Territory of a lion is always expanding. Be it with lionesses and more land, but also with more prey. Without a strong hold on the lion's territory, the lion can lose his lionesses, land, and prey. This is why the lion will patrol his territory and socialize with all who are under him. Remember, everybody wants to be the king. The territorial aspect is complimented by his ferocity in word and stance, but must maintain balance of respect among his territory or the fear will eat the territory inside out. The lion must always be aware of enemies within his kingdom and those outside who want what he already has.

The lion must have dignity, without dignity comes the inability to make a decision that will be moral with those in his territory. There is an inbred morality in any society, the lion maybe an amoral predator, but those in his kingdom are not. So, dignity is required to oversee those within the society that he has set up. The lion also knows that with proper manipulation he can use the morals of his people to accomplish certain amoral goals by building an unjust enemy. The lion must keep in mind that even an enemy must be treated with some dignity or he'll push his people too far and they will leave or revolt.

Know that both are equally feared, and then please take the time to study why they are feared. This is a basic overview of both symbolic animals as they pertain to Father Ahriman. The other animalistic symbol that I did not speak about is that Father Ahriman has the feet of a vulture. I suggested that one should look into that symbol as well. You may find a hidden treasure that is guarded by the serpent. Remember, the Persians and modern day Iranians have serious trouble with shades of grey, but they are well honed in the black and white.

Step 1

Respect all life because it can be converted to an advantageous opportunity if you understand its nature. You must first understand your own nature before you can understand another's.

Know that death and blood attract druj (general term for demons) but sacrifice is not an acceptable form to summon druj. To explain myself, we use a live female altar and one menstruating woman can have an entire village infiltrated with druj. What more attracting power do you need than a menstruating woman on the altar? Remember, at our base animal nature, men are sexually attracted to the smell of a menstruating woman. This should show that using a menstruating woman on the altar calls in the druj and brings forth bio/adrenal energy needed in ritual.

There are 3 ways to tap into the reptilian mind: fear, anger, and sex. These 3 emotions release adrenaline, and that's what gives the energetic push from all that are attending. Since most magic ritual in other magical schools of practice is solitary, you find that some schools of magic sacrifice living creatures to attain the proper adrenal energy that it takes to press the desire into the collective consciousness. This is a valid practice that is protected by the U.S Supreme Court, but I don't see a need for this practice when the reptilian brain can be tapped in a more sophisticated way. That is why in our rituals we use a menstruating woman and music that continues to push the proper emotion throughout the ritual.

If you ritualize the concept of sacrifice, then you will use this same concept in your life. This is way you see Christian folks being dubbed into sacrificing money, food, and their own lives. Also, ritualizing this concept in a physical form, can lead into human sacrifice which is illegal in most countries. This practice can also lead one into being able to sacrifice one's own family to accomplish a given goal. According to the mirror test, if that is in your nature, go for it but know I will not practice with such an individual. Those who are without are prey period, but your family and your fellow Ahrimanists are not your prey. Pour all your love and cherishment unto these people and expel all your anger and fear on those who are without a.k.a the herd.

Since we have established that the herd is our prey, and that will not sacrifice them, we will use lesser magic on them to attain our desires from them. Lesser magic requires one to understand the nature of their prey, but before you understand the nature of others you must understand your own nature. The way one does this is through testing yourself in different ways and paying attention to your own self as you conduct your daily life. An example of testing oneself is to stay up as many days that you can and watch how you react to people and how they react to you. Plus, deep study can press your limits as you learn a subject thoroughly. Once you know your own nature and limits, then you can read and direct another into what you would like them to do.

The purpose of lesser magic is to get folks to do what you want them to do. If you go around sacrificing yourself or others, you will eventually lay waste to yourself or run out of prey to attain your desires. It's like advertising; ads are designed to capture your emotion and imagination. These things are under the ads control, you subconsciously do exactly what the ad directs you to do: buy the product, join the military, or even who to vote for. The folks who design these ads are well aware of human nature and use it to their full advantage. So, why don't you? Take advantage of the life around you and respect it because you never know which one might turn out to be an enemy that is aware of what you're doing.

Those who are without should be enveloped into your veil as cast by the nature of the Serpent.

Earlier, the hypnotizing eyes of the serpent was lightly discussed along with deceit being another main attribute of the serpent. Since man is the only species that preys on its own species, let see how it can be done legally without sacrificing self or others. As discussed in Step 1, advertisers use this method to sell their products and so forth to attain profit. Profit is the purpose of growing and expanding a business. Thus the business owner using profits lives a better life. The basis for this type of philosophy can be found within Ayn Rand's books. If businesses sacrificed profits or customers, it would effectively die.

Just as businesses use commercials, slogans, and catch phrases to infiltrate your subconscious; you can use the same weapons of deceit on those who are without. Businesses stretch the truth and outright lie about things to get people in their doors. The special little trick is to tell people what they want to here. Nobody wants to hear the truth because the truth doesn't set you free. It normally only causes pain and discomfort. Example, most fast food joints say the use 100% beef. They fail to tell you that they inject all kind of preservatives and other chemicals that are bad for you. They also use the sickest and most cancerous cows for their meat. Do you think ingesting cancerous meat filled with chemicals is healthy? They say we serve 100% American beef that's never frozen. Really, then how did they deliver it cross country without it expiring? This is a billion-dollar business that attains quite a bit of profit. By the way, those chemicals in the meat cause a slight euphoria so an addiction to their product is made. Thus, repeat business, sounds similar to a crack dealer.

Here enters one of the amoral parts of Ahrimanism, if your prey is to choose you over another predator, you must offer something that is addicting. If you always tell your prey what they want to hear, then you should be deceiving them most of the time. When you use deceit along with hypnotism to manipulate your prey, you are casting a veil over their eyes. This veil needs a lot of personal attention, and the more you wish to get this person to do, the more time it will take from your personal life. It would be in your best interest to set your goals and plans up before you start any project such as this.

There are also little tricks one can use to make any interaction with people go smoothly. I highly suggest that one should study body language, sales techniques, and interrogation techniques as well. These should crack the surface of how lesser magic is used. Deep study and practice with these tools helps with the perfection of the art. The other piece that lots of magicians miss is the command to look.

Just as Father Ahriman is represented by the Serpent and the Lion, one should be able to fluidly adjust between the two in any situation.

As a predator in society you must be able to read your prey and the situation around you, as this is always ever changing. Chaos is where everything tries to return. Learning to read people and your environment will help you to determine which characteristics that you should use to your advantage in that place and time. The best way to attain this feel is to become relaxed but aware. Maintain this mental attitude as observe all aspects of your surroundings and listen to all the different background noises as well. Smell your environment, the sense of smell holds emotional memory the strongest. Then listen to your gut and emotions that you are feeling with that gut reaction.

Take time to realize that majority of modern society is setup to foster people's emotional states to attain their money. These stores are setup to appeal to all senses. Certain smells, colors, and symbols are used to attain these means. So you must learn to use these environments to your advantage. If you're in a coffee shop, would it be advantageous to act like a lion? No, a brash attitude would be frowned upon. Remember, we must still get along in society to a point that our predatory actions don't fall back upon us.

Let's say we are still in the coffee house. The smell is that of coffee, what type of reaction does that create? I'm sure there is some upbeat folk or jazz music playing, how is this influencing the environment? Is it during a rush or slow time? Plus how many people are fluctuating in and out of the bathrooms? Do all these details matter, yes! Being aware of your environment will help you to plan the proper strategy when you approach your prey. Is it in your best interest to be the cock of the walk, or to approach with quiet dignity?

Let's change the environment, a night club. The environment is filled with adult beverages, tobacco, loud music, drugs, and people with lowered inhibitions; this is a potentially explosive situation. That's why there are many bouncers and what is known as coolers, coolers are the bouncers' supervisors. These folks put out the "fires" before they spread into group issues. Taking into account as to what we're dealing with, the concept of Lion should seem the most appropriate. Either way you must protect yourself, and if you brought a date you must protect them from other predators as well.

When people are inebriated, they are much closer to their primitive animal state because inhibitions are lowered. If people take the right mix of drugs can make them potentially dangerous. It you project confidence then most people won't mess with you, but there is always foolish people around. Let's flip the switch that fool has decided to challenge you. You become larger than life and 10 foot tall. While acting like they lion, you should be positioning yourself toward a bouncer. This should be serpent behavior. Let's face it; in today's society allowing the bouncer to put hands on the fool is the better decision. Who wants to go court for an assault and battery charge when you could stand your ground like a lion and deceive the fool like a serpent by leading him to the bouncer? Even if you started it, the bouncer won't know, thus using the serpent again. Be fluid between both concepts as they will help you throughout your life's decisions.

Remember Father Ahriman in all things because within His hands are the keys to the universe and the rod of undiluted wisdom.

As discussed in the Way of Ahriman, Melek Taus retrieved the keys to the universe for Father Ahriman. This means Father Ahriman has complete set of keys to both dualities of the universe. As part of the character inversion, the Zoroastrians claim that Father Ahriman is without knowledge and that Hormazd is all knowing. Put the slaves at ease so they follow you're plan. If only the slaves knew the truth, the fear it would beget, everything returns to chaos.

Also, remember Father Ahriman was born first and given the rod of undiluted wisdom and the blessing of being first born. That is why He ripped himself out of the womb of His mother. In the pursuit of power, Father Ahriman did what it took to attain that power. Let this be a lessoned learned. To attain power, you must be one minded at times to attain it, and compassion may have to be over looked to attain such things. Angra Mainyu does mean destructive spirit, remember that always.

The idea in science that all particles of matter are trying to reduce back to chaos from order should easily be observed throughout nature. One of the main perpetrators of this chaotic movement is natural disasters: earthquakes, tornados, hurricanes, floods, droughts, plague, famine, and infestation. These disasters inspire manmade disasters: war, enslavement, and destruction to the environment. One can cause the other, and manmade ones may have no cause other than a woman. Remember, Father Ahriman's starves you, so you will go get what you need or want by any means necessary and Father Melek Taus will inspire you with dreams and goals that you attain by any means. Never allow yourself to be pushed beyond your nature.

Be mindful in the fact that all things you do should have the "spirit" or idea of Father Ahriman behind it. You must also be aware of how for your willing to go to get the things you want and/or need. Allow Father Melek Taus to guide you and inspire you to attain goals that are available to you. Keep in mind what is probable and what is possible, there is a huge difference. We can attain anything, just figuring out how is always the issue.

As in Hell, we should amass power, strength, and pleasure. Never allow yourself to become drunk with any.

The most important power is self-power. Self-power is attained through self-knowledge, self-discipline, self-confidence, and self-respect. Pushing ones' limits has already been discussed and is a critical in self-knowledge. Self-discipline is an important part of this picture. This aspect of self, will teach you restraint. Why is restraint important? Refer back to the nature of the serpent. Meditation and nightly ritual will help to harness a sense of self-discipline by repeating the same steps and words over and over again. There will be times when you don't want to do this but you must press forward and do it anyway. If you're actually sick or injured, then skip a night or 2 but don't go beyond that unless you have too. Part of self-discipline is facing yourself with all your excuses and pressing forward through all the emotions and other issues.

Learning to conquer you will teach discipline and what is known as actively waiting "patience." In Traditional Ahrimanism the concept of patience is known as actively waiting because patience is like ignoring people till they come around to acceptable behavior. This is R.H.P concept that has no bearing into what we are doing, so we look into a concept that is similar but has different reasoning behind it. Actively waiting is observing and studying a person or group. Poke the dog with a stick to see how it reacts; learn its nature to plan your best attack strategy. Learning this skill will boost your confidence.

Another way to boost your self-confidence is to get involved in some type of physical activity. Stay away from lone activity such as walking or running. Get involved in something that give you time to learn a physical skill that you learn with a group of people. This will enlighten you to a myriad of things that include social structure, being a chameleon, and physical skill that you can use. Martial Arts, dance, and/or group music are excellent ways to build self-confidence because you monitor your own progression versus others and find ways to always improve. Self-discipline and self-respect will also be built from this as well.

Why is self-respect so important? If you can't respect yourself, how can you respect others? This is simple basic things like shower, brush your hair and teeth, and wash your clothes. Learn to take care of yourself and your personal environment. Take care of your ritual tools and chamber. Take pride in all that you do and it will show. This will influence others to come to your side. People like being around other people who are confident, clean, and clear headed. Project that image into your prey to build false confidence into them.

Even as you amass personal power and strength along with power of influence over other people, be mindful that you maintain a level head. If you allow your ego to blowup into thinking you are the all-knowing source, you will become blind to what is going on around you. This will become your greatest weakness because flattery will easily destroy you. Becoming drunk with strength and power makes it to distract you with pleasure.

Pleasure comes in many forms and each person enjoys different pleasures in different ways. We as a species are self-destructive, lazy, and weak. Every person has their personal poison that has to be taken in doses because if they don't the pleasure will take over. Indulge in all your animal desires so they never take over your life. This doesn't only include sex. If you maintain a self-balance, it's that much harder for you to become prey yourself. Remember, the most dangerous enemy is the one you never see coming, that enemy is most likely the one providing you with the most pleasure.

While we are upon this Earth, never forget that our actions and reputation speaks louder than any words. Ask, what can be destroyed to create something better.

Your past actions will precede everything that you do. People love to talk about other people's achievements and follies. They also like to spread negative information about other folks very quickly. Remember, if someone can elevate themselves by another's downfall, they will. Then there are the assholes who will take the whole thing down with them out of spite. Actions do speak louder words, but nothing speaks louder about a person than their reputation. Your reputation can also be a double edge sword because if you go against your reputation it will be attacked with the up most ferocity.

The crowd is fickle; nothing is truer than that. When you're winning, they will be behind you and if you're entertaining while winning, admirers you will attain. Hope you got what it takes to keep them on your side. As soon as you make a mistake, there will be a hater to point it out to everybody. This person is just trying to gain notoriety off of your fame. These folks can make or break you if they are allowed to continue an assault against you. Most of these haters are shut down by continued positive actions on your part, but if you head into a downward spiral they will kick you down it faster and harder than you ever wanted to go. These hecklers do influence the crowd's ability to be fickle, but if your reputation is strong and your actions remain strong then the haters influence will remain weak. If people are talking about you, you amass power.

With power comes a group of people that you will have to work and deal with. As the crowd is fickle, so is this group. You will have haters within this group as well. Some are just mouths running while others are plotting against you. Those closest to you will make or break you. Your reputation will attract certain types of people and most are there to help, but be weary of the one who wants to take all you built for their own. Please also be mindful of those who become disillusioned and spiteful will see the walls crashing down around them, and they will try to take everybody down with them. If you maintain your strong reputation, you can always rebuild.

If you go against your reputation with a big mistake, you may not be able to recover. When you go against all that you built, the viper may take your thing or the disillusioned will burn the whole thing to the ground. Those who are with can change fickly and either goes with the new leader or helps burn you down. Never build your power base against your nature because you will not always be able to play the role. People will see you at your base nature one way or another and make their decision based on that. Lie in the beginning and be ready to deal with that down the road and hope your haters don't eat you alive. Now you know how to destroy someone's thing to create something better.

Father Ahriman expects us to gain knowledge and to forever press forward forging ourselves. We are never expected to go beyond our nature, just press our limits.

Knowledge is the beginning of power; knowledge can be useless if you don't use it or exercise it. The best way to gain knowledge is to read or observe other people. Let's take body language for example. It's good to read as many books on the subject in many different areas of this topic's uses. With the study of body language there are different types of study that should be looked into: basic, attracting the opposite sex, attracting the same sex, sales, interviewing, and interrogating. Through studying these different areas of the subject, you should run across videos that help explain what is happening with each part. These videos should cover the observation part.

Now you must evaluate all the information you just took in. There should have been ideas that you will embrace without question. There should be some that you're not sure of but will try. Then there should be some techniques that you will not even touch because they go against your nature, or do they? Here is where limits are to be pushed. Pushing your limits helps you gain self-knowledge which leads to power. It's up to you to decide how far down the rabbit hole you will go and how much you choose to learn and practice. Just don't go beyond your nature and go into the guilt cycle that the R.H.P loves to force people into.

When facing an enemy, be fluid with the dictates of the Serpent and the Lion. Know which is most advantageous, the assassin or the warrior. Both are highly trained and equally effective in the right situation.

The warrior is a highly-trained killer that is trained in many diverse arts. Weapons training goes without saying, there are also other arts they must learn: marching, horseback riding, swimming, siege, armor mending, first aid, capture, and etc. The assassin is highly trained as well. Obviously weapons and to include: chemistry (explosives and poisons), sabotage, infiltration, traps, covert ops, subterfuge, disguise, camouflage, first aid, and etc. The biggest strength and the biggest weakness with the warrior is the fact they operate in highly trained groups, with some independent survival training. The same with the assassin they operate alone or in small groups, this is the greatest strength and weakness because if they're ever found out…

When engaging the enemy in battle, which is more advantageous to the outcome of victory, the warrior or the assassin? It is best to use both in the proper way to exploit the weakness of the enemy. The fools rush in with the warrior is not the best idea; you're throwing dice not knowing what possible outcomes could happen or how to adjust fluidly in the heat of battle. Your first move should be to attain knowledge of the enemy. The assassin would be best to attain inside knowledge of the enemy, and a scout would be best to attain knowledge around the enemy. Knowledge is the beginning of power.

Once both have reported all the information they have gathered, it's up to you to assess the information given to you. Keep in the people you sent to gather said information and their disposition toward you as a leader. Have they shown error or laziness in the past or how likely did they give their position away? Also take into account how likely they are to sell you out to the enemy. These are all things you must take in account when you are in said pursuit. Be ready to change your position and how you are going to attack or re-attack as it becomes necessary.

Find your enemies weakness and exploit it. If the enemy runs the thing with complete authority, its best to cut the head off the snake and watch the whole thing crumble. The assassin is best for this type of scenario. If the enemy has multiple leaders who can always take command, assassinating the head is a bad idea because another head will grow in its place. So, a well-planned battle could be best. There are a million different types of strategy to deploy in this situation, it's up to you to evaluate the situation and use the right tool to accomplish the job in the most effective way.

Fill those who are without, with false sense of pride and security. Then when you call upon Chaos for Order, they will follow.

Flattery is worth more than gold. We live in a society were compliments are not given freely, but insults are. This leaves an open weakness for most people and an easy way in for you to begin. The more you compliment someone, the more they will come to like you. Since you are the only one who gives compliments away freely, you are the one that is kept around. The thing you have to remember is that all you're doing is acting, playing a part. Only you need to know the real you.

As an actor, you don't invest yourself into the prey. You must learn to objectify those who are without. This is a psychological technique that allows us to see humans and animals as objects. This is to keep us from forming an emotional bond with those who are without, but be warned, if allow yourself to become drunk with power you may step into doing illegal activities. The ability to maintain your ego and an objectified view is a difficult balancing act that you must learn to cope with. Also keep in mind, not to take yourself beyond your nature and don't push your prey past theirs. If this does occur, you better start a back pedal to get things out of the guilt arena.

Keeping the warning in mind, let's look at how we develop a false sense of pride and security into those who are without. Emotions are more contagious than viruses. If you push an emotion out and on to another person, they will feel that way also. That is why people

145

whom are excited about something get other people involved easily. If you combine flattery and high emotions that push into the person, what do you think has developed? Over time you should have developed someone with a false ego that is based around your flattery and a sense of security when they are around you. So, asking them a favor should be easy. I bet they will do it.

As time continues, your favors can increase in value. Avoid money, unless you're recommending attaining something for you or your interest. If sexual favors are involved, be mindful of the person's marital status and whether or not if that will come around to haunt you. If cheating is involved, then guilt will be as well. Plus, you will have the spouse to deal with. Again, don't push people beyond their nature. Beyond that the prey should be come putty in your hands over time. As you pull the strings, a balanced must be maintained.

By now it should be obvious that if you want change to happen, you need convince those with power to make that change. Hopefully you have preplanned your prey and the goals you wish to attain with such. Sure, some things will change on the fly; so long as the end goal is attained does it matter? You can't control all the factors that occur throughout life or with another person. Just learn to maneuver around them to press forward to the goal.

Through proper flattery and a well-built sense of security, you should be able to invoke the chaos you need to change the situation to match your plan. After the chaos, order should fall in the way you direct it. You just need the proper people with the power to make these changes occur. Once you have them under your spell, all should be easy. Rule with flattery and deception. Some fear is good, but don't use it as your main power play because people will revolt against fear.

Just as Father Ahriman remains in the darkness of the Earth, so shall we retreat to the darkness to attain His wisdom and conduct His rituals. For Melek Taus lights the way!

As the Zoroastrians believe, the druj and other demons are free to roam about at night in the dark. That is why they remained inside with a fire burning and dogs around. Originally evil was not seen as fire, but as water. For deep in the murky depths of the water is where evil dwelt, or deep in the caves filled with darkness. Where do serpents, scorpions, and other physical druj live? In the darkness where they are separated from light and are free to conduct themselves as they see fit.

If we are to attain Father Ahriman's wisdom, then must retreat from the light and join Him in the darkness. Your ritual chamber or area set aside should be dark, and you should try to keep it in the darkness as best you can. This is a sacred space dedicated to Father Ahriman, Melek Taus, and you. The only illumination within the room during any type of ritual, if the room is used for other practical purposes; please try to use only artificial light. You're trying to maintain a sense of darkness that is inviting to the denizens of Hell.

Remember, Hell is not a lake of fire where sinners roast on an open flame. It is a spiritual dimension separated from the tyranny of enslavement. Here in the realm of the physical, it is our free choice to decide which path we dedicate ourselves to or whatever else we decide to do with our lives. So, the everlasting presence of the slave-master and his servants will be present here in the physical. This is why we create our ritual chamber in the likeness of Hell and its darkness.

Envision a dark watery cave deep in the depths of the Earth, filled with awesome ancient monoliths of spiritual knowledge. You may also find other souls that you may or may not have known or heard of in life. There may also be minor demons around watching and playing if you will. Just as you have your own personality, so do they. Some will work with you, deceive you, ignore you, and etc. You must treat them with same caution that you would with new people. In this chaos there is an illuminating light, Melek Taus.

Melek Taus was created from the destruction of an eagle. Father Ahriman answered Hormazd's challenge to create something good by this act. The Peacock Angel is the demi-god assigned to rule over this world. He enlightens us with the black flame and communicates to us Father Ahriman's great spiritual plan. He can move between all realms and shares ruling the ages of time with the other Daevas. Melek Taus is the head Daeva. Melek Taus is our guardian and guide in this world.

Never trust any man's dictates or words because every man has his own agenda. Ask yourself if your agenda fits theirs.

This seems to be self-evident to most folks, sometimes it's not. Throughout these lessons you have been pointed toward the basics of Lesser Magic. By now it should be obvious that I'm pointing in a direction for self-study. Don't rely on other people be a sole source of anything. There are knowledgeable people out there, but they worked for that knowledge and expect that you do the same. Some people will tell you a bunch of garbage to gain and maintain control over you.

Let's say somebody is attempting to use Lesser Magic on you. First thing is to learn how to spot that they are using this method on you. Then you find your personal way to deflect the attempts. Once this is established, you find out what this person is trying to accomplish. Then you must ask yourself, "Does this fit into my agenda as well?"

Ahrimanism places quite a heavy load on people, it makes them think about what they wish to accomplish. After that is thought-out, you must set goals and a plan to accomplish these goals. These are reality based concepts that should be understood. We don't wait around for things to be handed to us. You must work for things you wish to accomplish and if someone else gets involved that isn't conducive to your goal, get rid of them.

There is a form of compassion that is discussed by one of my favorite and famous samurai philosopher.

Musashi's understanding of compassion should be looked at and taken into consideration. To simplify this understanding, know your enemy better than you know yourself. Thus allowing you the ability to either forgive or destroy them at will. This type of mature thinking is another missing piece of the puzzle for most folks.

Man has made great advances in his understanding of the physical universe, but only Father Ahriman knows the spiritual universe.

Quantum Physics have opened quite a door to a physical understanding of the Universe. Many Black Magicians study this new concept of scientific understanding with an understanding of Greater Magic. This study is truly a worth wild idea. If something works and you don't understand why, is it worth pulling it apart to learn how it works? In other words, would you pull your car apart to learn how it works? Also, would you be able to put it back together again?

Greater Magic is a spiritual manipulation over the physical. We are both flesh and spirit and they fuel one another. This makes each of us a generator and an antenna. Males are normally stronger generators and females are stronger antenna. We all know that in reality, there are effeminate men and masculine women. So, the roles can be reversed if necessary.

This is the core of Greater Magic, allowing both to charge the change in reality that's to be seen. The group that surrounds the core supplies extra energy to fuel the ritual. Once sex act is started, by the core and/or everybody around them, is how you penetrate in the energy exchange with Ahriman. All parties involved in the sex act should hold the image of the projected change until climax has occurred. The burst of energy from climax sends the change into the collective conscious.

The sex act allows both parties to open completely and allow Father Ahriman into the exchange. This is how we ask for His help to create the change, and our flesh energy is exchanged for His spiritual energy. With the backing of Him, the higher the chances for the change to occur. Do we need to strip this process down to the atomic and sub-atomic level for an ability to use it? Can you drive your car without knowing auto mechanics?

Allow Father Ahriman to direct the spiritual side of your life. He empowers and directs our spiritual energy towards our goals, which is His great spiritual plan. The most powerful spiritual weapon is belief, not faith. Faith is weakness that allows for dogma to encramp your thinking. Belief allows for your inner strength to be tapped and energize you for your goals.

Always know that you are a part of Father Ahriman's Great Spiritual Plan. Whether or not, if he is testing you with fire or hardening you with ice.

Know that life is always filled with problems and issues that can be vexing or quite disheartening. Question being, how many of these did you bring upon yourself? Accepting responsibility for the things you do is very important piece. If you accept full control of your life, then you must accept responsibility for aspects of your life. Be it negative, positive, or outright neutral.

The goals that you set to attain your end goal will have problems that need to be solved. Some will require fire, so that you can be molded and have resilience. While others will require ice, to harden and solidify your belief in Father Ahriman's Great Spiritual Plan. Your journey through life to attain your goals will teach you many lessons with both fire and ice. Learn from all of these, mistakes are made to be learned from not to destroy your ego.

Society demands perfection, this is completely stupid. As you make your way through life mistakes will be made and most should allow for a full recovery. If there is one that doesn't then relocation should be considered. Just believe that any mistake or problem can be solved and it can. You will have to work and figure out how.

Self-respect is the most important thing in life. With self-respect you will gain self-confidence, self-knowledge, and power. Just as you should respect all living things, you should respect yourself more than anything else in this Universe. This life is for you to create it the way you want it. Ever press forward to your goals and desires, for sin drives man to Godhood.

The Watch Towers of Reality hold both angelic and demonic forces. Within each Watch Tower there are gates that can be opened with different keys. Unlocking different Towers can be puzzling, but it's really simple. The problem is which one of the 57 cacodemons is the proper one to call.

This is where self-transformative ritual can begin. If one were to call the 19th key nightly using a different cacodemon every night, one might get to know what each demon is for. Then play connect the dots the Infernal Gods, Daevas, Dews, and cacodemons. Also, review each Enochian Key and what it is for. Use the key/s that matches the attributes of the mentioned entities. The Enochian Keys release the gates of the Watch Towers and lets out some of the most powerful spiritual creatures known. The keys also throw open the locks of the conscious, subconscious, and collective consciousness so that the desire can be willed into existence.

The Enochian Keys

The First Key

The First Enochian Key represents Ahriman's Law. It states the incorporation of Earthly rules and theologies that give power to the people bold enough to recognize it as it is.

The First Key

(Enochian)

Ol sonf nonci gohe Coronzon, a micalz vors
Thahnaotahe od donasdogamatatastos! I soba
zol oro I ta nazpsad. Od graa ta luciftias ial
por; Ds holq qaa nothoa zimz, od commah gi ta
nohbloh ohorela de caba, Ton!, sa zonrensg
ialpor napta de ananael. Gi farzmg faaip od
surzas gi adna Coronzon, na apila homtoh,
soba gevamma ge, lu uls adgtip trian, Ds
loholo ca vep I zomd de g poamalzad, sa
bogpa aaf gi ta prap de apila! Zacare ca sa
zamran! Odo cicles qaaon! Zorge pugo ol, lap
zirdo lel! Hoarth de tol iadnah Coronzon,
bospa donasdogmatatastos.

The First Key

(English)

I reign over you, says Ahriman, with power over Earth and Hellfire! In whose hands the sun is as a sword. The moon as a bright burning fire; who measures your garments in the midst of my vestures and trusseth you as the palms of my hands; and brighten your garments with the light of Hellfire! I made you laws to govern all! And delivered a flaming sword of wisdom. You lifted up your voices and swore your obedience to Ahriman, that lives in triumph, whose beginning is not, nor end cannot be, who shines as a flame, in the midst of your palace, and reign amongst you as the balance of life! Move therefore and appear! Open the mysteries of your creation! Be friendly unto me, for I am the same!- the servant of all knowing Ahriman, ruler of Hellfire!

The Second Key

The Second Key is a charging ritual tools. This brings the power of Hell and Ahriman to all your magical items.

The Second Key

(Enochian)

Adgt upaah zong faaip sald?; ca Rzion Nrzfm!
Sobam donasdogmatatastos izazaz pia dph.
Casarma abramg tatalho paraaclecla qa ta lor
lsq turbs ooge doalim. Givi chis lusd orri!
Micalp chis bia ozongon; lap noan trof cors ta
ge, oq manin tolmicalzo Coronzon! Torzulp,
gohe L. Zacar ca c noqod! Zamran micalzo, od
ozazm givi uran laiad lap zir a Coronzon na
apila paid!

The Second Key

(English)

Can the wings of the wings hear your voices of wonder? O you Gods of Fire! Whom the Hellfire frames in the depth of my jaws! Whom I have prepared as cups for a wedding or as flowers in their beauty for the chamber of sin. Stronger are your feet than the barriers stone! Mightier are your voices than the manifold winds!, for you are become as a building such is not, save in the mind of the All-Powerful manifestation of Ahriman! Arise, says the first. Move therefore unto his servants! Show yourselves in power, and make men strong seer-of-things for I am Ahriman that live forever!

The Third Key

169

The Third Key shows human Leadership having power to establish dominance over mankind with Satanic magic.

The Third Key

(Enochian)

Micma!, goho Coronzon, zir comselh zien biah em londoh. Nors chis othil gigipah, undl chis ta puim, mospleth teloch. Quiin toltorg chisi chis ge, m ozien ds brgda od! Torzul I li eol balzarg, od aala em thiln netaab, dluga vomsarg lonsa capmiali vors homil cocasb, fafen izizop od miinoag de g netaab, vaun nanaeel panpir malpirg pild caosg. Noan unalah balt od vooan. Doioap Coronzon, goholor zamran! Micma!, iehusoz cacaom, od dooain noar micaolz aaiom. Casarmg gohia: Zacar! Gohulor!, od imvamar pugo, plapli ananael do qaan!

The Third Key

(English)

Behold!, says Ahriman, I am a circle whose hands stands the nine kingdoms. Six are the seats of living breath, the rest are as sharp sickles, or the Horns of Death. Therein the creatures of the Earth are and are not, except in mine own hands which sleep shall rise!, In the First. I made you stewards, and placed you in the nine seats of Government. Giving unto every one of you power successively over the true ages of time, so that from the highest vessels and the corners of your governments, you might work my power, pouring down the fires of life and increase continually on Earth. Thus you are to become the skirts of justice and truth. In Ahriman's name, rise up! Show yourselves! Behold!, his mercies flourish, and his name is become mighty among us. In whom we say: Move! Ascend!, and apply yourselves unto us! The partakers of His secret wisdom in your creation!

The Fourth Key

The Fourth Key is to call people

to Ahriman. Sons of Adam only.

The Fourth Key

(Enochian)

Othil lasdi babage, od dorpha, gohol: g chis ge
avavago comp priaz ds bogpa viu diu?
Casarm: ag brin cormpo, crp l, casarmg viu
croodzi chis od ugeg, capimali uml cor a
homin, od lonshin gnay biah elo a em! Torgu!,
nor quasahi, od caosga bagle zir enay,
Coronzon, which I od apila paid! Dooaip
Coronzon, Zacar!, od zamran obelisong, rest
Coronzon aaf nor malop!

The Fourth Key

(English)

I have set my feet in the South, and have looked about me, saying: Are not the thunders of increase those which reign in the second angle? Under whom none hath yet numbered, but one, in whom the second beginnings of things are and wax strong, successively adding the number of time, and their powers doth stand as the first of the nine! Arise!, you sons of pleasure, and visit the Earth: for I am the Lord, Ahriman, which is and lives always! In the name of Satan, move!, and show yourselves as pleasant deliverers, that you praise Ahriman among the sons of men!

The Fifth Key

The Fifth Key gives power to the

Satanic Priest and magician for

the purpose of misdirection!

The Fifth Key

(Enochian)

Vohim sapah zimii d diu od noas to qting
levith mong, ucim osf mire coasg, od faonts
piripsol ta pild bljorax quasb a molap. Mire
soba ol amizpi nazarth, Na piamol, od dlugar
zizop zlida coasgi tol torgi. Z chis esiasch a I ta
vin, od iaod thild ds gnonp drilpi cora pild
ialor hubar, soba cormfa chis ta la, uls, od q
cocasb! Ca, niis gi od darbs qaas. F etharzi od
bliora. Iaial ednas cicles; lap? Coronzon ge
Enay, Ton-Saga!

The Fifth Key

(English)

The Mighty sounds have entered into the third angle and are become as rotten cattle, smiling with discord upon the Earth, and dwelling in the brightness of heaven as continual comforters to the destroyers of man. Upon whom I fastened the pillars of gladness, the lords of righteous, and gave them vessels to water the Earth with her creatures. They are the brothers of the First and the Second, and the beginning of their own seats which are garnished with great numbers of continued burning lamps, whose number are as the First, the ends, and the contents of time! Therefore, come you and obey your creation. Visit us in peace and comfort. Conclude us receivers of your mysteries; for why? Ahriman our Lord is the All-one!

The Sixth Key

The Sixth Key gives power to the
establishment of the Overseers
and the Church of Ahriman
by Ahriman and the Infernal
Legions of Hell!

The Sixth Key

(Enochian)

Gah s diu em, micalzo pilzin
donasdogamatatastos; sobam el harg mir
samvelg od obloc babalon, dlugar malpry ar
caosgi, od chis netab od miam ta viu od D.
Darsar solpeth bien; brita, od zacom ge
micalzo, sobha ath trian luiahe od ecrin
Coronzon qaaon.

The Sixth Key

(English)

The spirits of the fourth angle are nine, mighty in the firmament of Hellfire; whom the first has planted as a torment to the righteous and a garland to the wicked, giving unto them fiery darts to winnow the Earth, and the nine continual workmen; and are government and continuance as the second and the third. Therefore harken unto my voice; I have talked to you, and I move you in power and presence, whose works shall be a song of honor and the praise of Ahriman in your creation.

The Seventh Key

The Seventh Key is to allow oneself

To become filled with the worldly

desires. To celebrate being humam.

The Seventh Key

(Enochian)

Raas I salma babalond, oerimi aao donasdogamatatastos quiin Coronzon butmon; od inoas paradial casarmg ugear chirlon; od zonac luciftian, corsta vaul zirn tol hami. Soba londoh od miam chis ta o od es umadea od pi bliar, othil quasahi, Zacar! Zamram!, oecrimi caosgi od omicaolz aai om. Bagel papnor I dlugam, od umplif ugegi bigliad.

The Seventh Key

(English)

The East is a house of harlots, singing praises
among the Hellfire of the First glory where
Ahriman hath opened His Mouth; and they
become as living dwellings in whom the
strength of man rejoices; and they are
appareled with ornaments of Brightness, such
as work wonders on all creatures. Whose
kingdoms and continuance are 3rd and 4th
strong towers and palaces of comfort, the seats
of pleasure and continuance. O you servants
of pleasure, Move!, Appear!, sing praises unto
Earth and be mighty amongst us. For that to
this remembrance is given power, and our
strength waxes strong in our comforter.

The Eighth Key

The Eighth Key acknowledges

Melek Taus rising back unto Earth

!

The Eighth Key

(Enochian)

Bazm elo I ta donasdogamatatastos oln avabh
naz, casarmg uran chis ugeg; ds abramig
doalim, goho Coronzon: soba mian trian ta
lolcis vovin. Irgil chis da ds paaox busd
caosgo, ds chis, od ip uran teloah cacrg salman
loncho od vovin carbaf? Chirlan! Bagel
momao siaion od donasdogamatatastos
Coronzon I, as, momar ip! Niis! Zamran!,
ciaofi Caosgo, od bliors cors I ta abramig!

The Eighth Key

(English)

The midday of the first is as the third Hellfire
made of hyacinth pillars, in whom the elders
are becoming strong; says Ahriman; whose
long continuance shall be as bucklers to
Leviathan doth sink? Rejoice! For the crowns
of the temple and the Hellfire of Ahriman that
is, was, and shall be crowned are not divided!
Come forth! Appear!, to terror of the Earth,
and to the comfort of such as are prepared!

The Ninth Key

The Ninth Key warns against any type of addiction. This weakens the master into enslavements of false desires that own him.

The Ninth Key

(Enochian)

Micaolz bransg prgel napta ialor (ds efafafe qting, sobca upaah chis tatan od tranan balye), ta las ollor gnay limlal. Amma chiis sobca Madrid za chis! Ooanoun chis aviny drilpi caosgin, od butmoni parm zumvi cnila. Daziz ethamz a childao, od mire daziz chi pidiai collal. Ulcinin a sobam ucim. Bagel? Na Baltoh chirlan par! Niiso, od ofafare, bagel a cocasb I cors ca unig blior!

The Ninth Key

(English)

A mighty guard of fire with a two edged
swords flaming (which contain vials of rotten,
whose wings are of wormwood and od
marrow salt), have set their feet in the moss of
the Earth, as rich man doth his treasure.
Cursed are they whose iniquities they are! In
their eyes are milestones greater than the
Earth, and from their mouths rain seas of
blood. Their heads are covered with
diamonds, and their heads are marble stones.
Happy is he whom they frown not. For why?
The Lord of Righteousness Come away, and
leave your vials, for the time is as such
required comfort!

The Tenth Key

The Tenth Key is to produce

a violent call of an avenging

curse against your enemies!

The Tenth Key

(Enochian)

Coraxo vonpho gnay page local, aziazior paeb
soba lilonon chis a salbrox virg oephan od
raclir maasi bagel caosgi, ialpon dosig od
basgim od oxex dazis siatris od salbrox cynxir
faboan. Unal chis const ds yor eors vohim
gizyax od matb plosi molvi, ds page ip, larag
om droln matorb cocasb L patralx yolci matb,
nomig monos olora gnay angelard. Ohio!
Ohio! Ohio! Ohio! Ohio! Ohio! Noib!, ohio
caosgon, bagel Madrid I, zirop, chiso drilpa.
Niiso! Crip ip vohim sapah!

The Tenth Key

(English)

The Thunders of wrath doth rest in the North, in the likeness of an oak whose branches are filled with sulphur nest of lamentation and weeping laid up for the Earth, which burn night and day and vomit out the heads of scorpions and live sulphur mingled with poison. These be the thunders that in an instant roar with a 100 mighty earthquakes and a 1000 as many surges, which rest not. Nor know any echoing time. One rock bring forth a 1000, even as the heart of man doth his thoughts! Woe! Woe! Woe! Woe! Woe! Woe! Yea!, woe be to the Earth, for her iniquity is, was, and shall be great! Come away! But not your mighty sounds!

The Eleventh Key

The Eleventh Key is for a funeral.

The Eleventh Key

(Enochian)

Micalzo oxiayal holdo od zirom o coraxo ds
zildar raasg. Vabzir camliax od bahal! Niiso
salman teloch!, od par aldon od noan casarman
holq, od par ag teloch ds comselh zong. Niisa!
Bagel abramg pi gi. Zacare, Ca, od zamran!
Odo cicle qaa zorge. Lap zirdo Coronzon,
hoath doalim na apila Paid!

The Eleventh Key

(English)

The mighty throne growled and there were five thunders which flew to the East. The Eagle spake and cried aloud: Come away from the house of death! And they gathered themselves together and became those who it measured, and they have no death which rides the circle winds. Come away! For I have prepared a place for you. Move therefor, and show yourselves! Unveil the mysteries of your creation. Be friendly unto me. For I am Ahriman, true worshipper of sin that lives always!

The Twelfth Key

The Twelfth Key is to curse

those who are miserable and

want you to be miserable as well.

The Twelfth Key

(Enochian)

Nonei ds sonf babage od chis hubaio tibibp, allar atraah od ef! Drix bransg donasdogamatatastos, ar Coronzon ovof, soba dooain aai I vonph! Zacar ca, zamran! Odo cicle qaa! Zorge, lap zirdo lel! Hoath Coronzon, Iaida donasdogamatatastos!

The Twelfth Key

(English)

O ye that reign in the South and are the
lanterns of sorrow, buckle your girdles and
visit us! Bring forth the guards of Hellfire, that
Ahriman may be magnified, whose name
among you is Wrath! Move therefore, and
appear! Open the mysteries of your creation!
Be friendly unto me, for I am the same! The
true worshipper of Ahriman, highest of
Hellfire!

The Thirteenth Key

The Thirteenth Key is for the lust
ritual. May be used to vex others
with sexual frustration.

The Thirteenth Key

(Enochian)

Napeai babagen, ds brin ooaona lring nonph
doalim, eolis oolog orsba ds chis affu! Micma!
Isro Coronzon oa lonshi. Ds I umd mai grosb!
Zacar od Zamran! Odo cicle qaa! Zorge lap
zirdo noco, hoath Coronzon, Iaida
donasdogamatatastos!

The Thirteenth Key

(English)

O ye swords of the South, which have eyes to
stir up the wrath of sin, making men drunken
which are empty! Behold! The promise of
Ahriman and His power, which is called
among you a bitter sting! Move and appear!
Unveil the mysteries of your creation! For I am
the servant of the same, the true worshiper of
Ahriman, highest king of Hellfire!

The Fourteenth Key

The Fourteenth Key is a call

for revenge against an enemy.

The Fourteenth Key

(Enochian)

Noromi pasbs mom manin, ds trint alco
Madrid drix ol Mica! Bial Coronzon; isro tox
ds um aai alca! Zacar ca!, zamran! Odo cicle
qaa! Zorge, lap zirdo lel! Hoath Coronzon,
Iaida donasgogamatatstos!

The Fourteenth Key

(English)

O ye sons and daughters of moss filled minds, which sit in judgment of the iniquities brought upon me. Behold! The voice of Ahriman; the promise of Him who called amongst you the true judge! Move therefore, and appear! Open your mysteries of your creations! Be friendly unto me, for I am the same! The true worshipper of Ahriman, the highest king of Hellfire!

The Fifteenth Key

The fifteenth Key is an understanding
that there are masters in the Right-hand
path that need to be recognized and ignored.

The Fifteenth Key

(Enochian)

Ils, tabaan l iaprt, casarnun upaahi chis qadah
mir oado caosgi orscor; omax monasci
"Baeovib" od emetgis hoxmarch! Zacar ca,
Zamran! Odo cicle qaa! Zorge lap, zirdo lel,
hoath Coronzon, Iaida donasdogamatatastos!

The Fifteenth Key

(English)

O thou, the governor of the first flame, under whose wings are the creators of torment that weave the Earth with dryness; that know the great name "Righteousness" and the seal of fear! Move therefore and appear! Open the mysteries of your creation! Be friendly unto me, for I am the same, the true worshipper of Ahriman, the highest king of Hellfire!

The Sixteenth Key

The Sixteenth Key is recognition of Ahriman's dichotomies and the Earth's Wonderful differences of beauty!

The Sixteenth Key

(Enochian)

Ils viu ialprt, salman balt, ds acroodzi busd od bliorax balit; ds insi caosg lusdan malpirgi; ds om od tlioc! Drilpa geh ils Coronzon Zilodarp! Zacar ca, zamran! Odo cicle qaa! Zorge, lap zirdo hoath Coronzon, Iaida donasdogamatatastos!

The Sixteenth Key

(English)

O thou second flame, the house of justice, which has
thy beginnings in glory and shalt comfort the just;
which walks upon the Earth with feet of fire; which
understands and separates creatures! Great art
though in Ahriman of the stretch-forth-and-conquer!
Move and appear! Open the mysteries of your
creations! Be friendly unto me, for I am the true
worshiper of Ahriman, the highest king of Hellfire!

The Seventeenth Key

The Seventeenth Key is for Melek Taus's enlightenment or mental vexation.

The Seventeenth Key

(Enochian)

Ils d iaprt! Soba upaah chis nanba zixlay dodsih, od brint gohed hubaro tustax ylsi; soba Coronzon; vonpo unph aldon dax od toatar! Zacar ca, zamran! Odo cicle qaa! Zorge, lap zirdo lel! Hoath Coronzon, Iaida donasdogamatatastos!

The Seventeenth Key

(English)

O thou third flame! Whose wings are thorns to
stir up vexation, and who has everlasting
living lamps going before thee; whose
Ahriman is wrath and anger-Gird up they
loins and harken! Move therefore and appear!
Open the mysteries of you creation! Be
friendly unto me, for I am the same, the true
worshipper of Ahriman, the highest king of
Hellfire!

The Eighteenth Key

The Eighteenth Key calls Melek Taus

Out of Hell and request His blessing!

The Eighteenth Key

(Enochian)

Ils micaolz olprit od ialprg bliors!, Ds odo basdir Coronzon ovoars caosgo! Casarmg laiad brints cafafam; ds I umd a q loadohi! "Ugear moz," od maoffas. Bolp como bliort pambt. Zacar ca, zamran! Odo cicle qaa! Zorge, lap zirdo lel! Hoath Coronzon, Iaida donasdogamatatastos!

The Eighteenth Key

(English)

O thou mighty light and burning flame of comfort!, that unveils the Glory of Ahriman to the center of the Earth! In whom the great secrets of truth have their abiding; that is called in thy kingdom! "Strength Through Joy," and is not to be measured. Be thou a window of comfort unto me. Move therefore and appear! Open the mysteries of your creation! Be friendly unto me, for I am the same! The true worshipper of Ahriman, the highest of Hellfire!

The Nineteenth Key

The Nineteenth key is the key that calls the Cacodemons forth into reality. This is the key that is called first.

Key of the 57 Cacodemons

(Enochian)

Quashi ds pragma do Pia, zirdo micalzo saanire Tplabc Zibra, fifis alca de vohim pugo nonce! Nostoah gohulim: Micma adoian a Coronzon, iaod a bliar, soba ooanoan chiso lucifitias aoiveae abraas gi lap taba Tplabc Zibra, od adphant damploz; tooat nonca nanaeel om de lrasd tofglo marb yarry Coronzon artrint a oxiayal, od goholor croodzi gohol: "Caosga, taboard pi saanir sa yrpoil a pi; adgmach a pi paid ors ba sa dodpal zylna. Zar parm aurelp doalim od ta qurlst, booapis. L nibm oucho symp; od ag toltorn mire tiobla lel. Cormfa dilzmo par aspian; sa par paradial, bams omaos. Conisbra od avavox, tonug. Orsca, noasmi tabges levithmong! Oucho oma cors! Baglen? Levithmong chiis ollor geh qting. L capimao ixomaxip, od ca cocasb gosa; baglen pi tianta a babalond, od faorgt darbs Choronzon. Torgu donasdogamatatastos. Zadzaczadlin camliax; Oadriax orocha aboupri! Tabaori priazar tabas! Adrpan cors tadobix. Yolcam priaziar coazoir, od quasb qting. Ripir, paaoxt saga cor; uml od prdzar cacrg aoiveae cormpt. Torzu! Zocar! Od zumran aspt sibs; Coronzon butmona, dsCoronzon surzas Tia padgze. Odo cicle qaa od ozazmu plapli IADANAMADA!

Key of the 57 Cacodemons

(English)

Oh ye pleasures which dwell in the first air, ye
are mighty in the parts of the Earth, and
execute the judgment of the mighty! Unto you
it is said: Behold the face of Ahriman, the
beginning of comfort, whose eyes are the
brightness of the stars which provided you for
the government of Earth, and her unspeakable
variety; furnishing you a power of
understanding to dispose of all things
according to the providence of Ahriman that
sits on the throne, and rose up in the beginning
saying: " The Earth, let her be governed by her
parts and let there be division in her, the glory
of her may be always drunken and vexed in
itself. Her course, let it run with the seeking of
sin; and as a hand maiden, let her serve them.
One Season, let it confound another; and let
there be no creature upon or within her be the
same. All her numbers, let them differ in their
qualities; and let there be no creature equal
with another! The reasonable creatures of the
Earth, and men, let them vex and weed out one

another; and their dwelling places, let them forget their names. The work of man and his pomp, let them be defaced. His buildings, let them become as caves for the beast of the fields! Confound her understanding with darkness! For why? The cattle that are men are rotten. One while let her be known, and unto another while a stranger; because she is the bed of a harlot, and the dwelling place of Ahriman the king. Arise Hellfire! Adam commands; The lower heavens beneath you, let them serve you! Govern those who govern! Cast down such as fall. Bring forth those that increase, and destroy the rotten. No place, let it remain in one number. Add and diminish until the stars be numbered. Arise! Move! And appear before the covenant of Ahriman's mouth, which Ahriman hath sworn unto us his vengeance. Open the mysteries of your creation, and make us partakers of the undefiled wisdom!

In the original set of Enochian Keys, the last key was known as the Key of the 30 Aethers. This should be obvious that originally the Enochian Keys were for weepy Right-handers. Also, the original keys were set as that, open the Watch Towers to summon angels. Through long study and deciphering the tablets and so forth, one finds the hidden cacodemons that live within. I have also rewritten the Enochian Keys, in both English and Enochian to match the idea of Traditional Ahrimanic Satanism. I worship and believe in God, Ahriman. The Guardian and Guiding Demi-God is Melek Taus. The black flame burns brighter than it has before. The Key of the 52 Cacodemons is the key that opens the whole thing. This opens the Watch Tower and lets out the Cacodemon you have summoned. The other keys communicate your intentions and lets out other forces and demons into reality. Also, Melek Taus can be called out into reality with this wonderful key, if you can figure it out. Maybe one day with enough energy and power Father Ahriman can come through back onto Earth. Here are the Cacodemons:

Aax Ato Erg Mop Pfm Xai

Adi Ava Ern Mto Pia Xcz

Agb Cab Exr Oap Piz Xdz

And Cac Hbr Odo Rad Xii

Aor Cam Hru Oec Rda Xom

Apa Cms Hua Oia Rpu Xoy

Apm Cop Mgm Ona Rrb Xpa

Ash Csc Mma Onp Rsi

Ast Eac Mou Rdi Rxp

Self-Transformative Rituals

The purpose of self-transformative rituals is to reprogram the subconscious mind. Every aspect of western culture is saturated with Judeo-Christian symbols, words, and images. This is done to reinforce their control on the subconscious mind. Psychology has proven that the subconscious mind is in control of almost all you do. The only aspect of the conscious mind that can fight it is will.

Remember, Father Ahriman is evil because he chooses to be. It is up to everybody, at one point in their life to choose which side they will stand on. The Judeo-Christian Empire sets everything up in its favor to keep as many people enslaved as it can. From the time you're born, to the time you die, you will interact with this monster in some shape or form. It surrounds every aspect of reality, and many a life was taken to make sure it was so.

Let's look at their sick little game. Up until you are about 13 years of age, the children are separated from adults at church. The reason for this is because the adults are being programmed on a subconscious level and the children are having their will broke. In many ways, the "church" trains children like dogs, reward "proper behavior" and punish "evil" behavior. Don't forget the boogieman that waits for them in the darkness of Hell.

"Candy for those who love Jesus," is heard throughout America! What if you don't love Jesus? You are shunned. Since man is naturally a social animal, guilt is then inspired. Guilt is the secret weapon to their control; no one wants guilt in their life. Then at 13 years old, we move from guilt into shame. The "Church" uses shame to replace will! The only reason why anyone would like to die or inhibit their natural desires is to fight off shame. Now here is their failsafe, your natural animal desires will have to eventually be sated. Then, as preprogrammed, you run back to the "church" for Jesus's forgiveness to alleviate the guilt and shame. You will pay huge amounts of money to be relieved of that nasty shame.

How that shame is shoved into your head is based the sin of the fallen seed. "Better for a man to fill the belly of a whore, than to have his seed fallen to the ground," is the old saying. This is lie that Christian Priests made up based on the Onan passage: "And Judah said unto Onan, Go in unto thy brother's wife, and marry her, and raise up see to thy brother. And Onan knew that the seed should not be his; and it came to pass, when he went unto his brother's wife, that he spilled it on the ground, lest that he should give seed to his brother. And the thing he did displeased the LORD: wherefore he slew him also." Genesis 38:8-10. I'm not sure how this reference was perverted to masturbation is the sin of the fallen seed, but we know the true reason. That is to keep people dependant upon the church because if people learned how to enjoy self-fulfillment, the shame game would lose full momentum. The nature of man is to be self-serving through self-fulfillment.

Let's also look into another reason why masturbation during adolescence is attacked so hard and easily used to instill shame. During this natural change, the adolescent already feels awkward about the changes that are occurring. Males are learning about the literal dick measuring game and are embarrassed by the fact they are getting erections for no reason. Females are learning that bigger breast attract more attention, but become embarrassed to the happenings of their menstrual cycle. These changes drive embarrassment, and if respected authority tells these adolescents that they should be ashamed of these natural changes, they will be because the fear of being shunned by their social circle known as the church which is the respected authority by their parents as well. Neither adolescent nor parent want to be shunned by the community because the natural understanding of safety in numbers.

The old edict of separating the sexes during adolescence has been used for centuries, and you still see it today in most churches. The males were separated and versed in hunting, war games, and/or sport. Along with the church's teachings, the coach is teaching not to masturbate or have sex because their legs will give out and their essences hold their strength. Funny thing is, during Roman times men would give each other fellatio to swallow each other's essence to attain the other's power. There is no scientific evidence to back any of this up, and the only reason for this is to keep males sexual frustrated to keep them aggressive.

While the females were separated from the males, specific things were taught. Some went back to gathering or gardening. The most prevalent that is still seen today is hand writing. Then as hand writing is perfected, creative writing is moved into. This helps with expressing the females need for adventure, and leads into reading as a habit. Now, the females' hands and fingers are cramped and their imagination is spent. This is how the monster of inhibition took over the lives of the adolescents by the "glorious" church. This controls and confounds the sexual nature, till marriage of course. Then sex isn't fun, it is to procreate more people, thus the cycle of money and people for the church.

As the adolescents reach adulthood, the weekly programming to keep the adult subdued continues. If there is an agenda that the clergy or state has, that will also be a part of the weekly programming as well. Zoroastrianism almost made it to state religion status by controlling how and when people defecated, the Catholic Church attacked the human base sexual nature. This allowed them to create that state religion that the Zoroastrians could not. Presently, the Baptists keep this moving forward under the same umbrella as the Catholics.

In order to combat the programming of any Christian church, TV, movies, media, and/or radio; here is a way that I'm providing. This way will not only reprogram your conscious mind, it will do the same for your subconscious. Now that an understanding of how society is programming you to be a certain way, it is up to you to choose what entertainment you indulge in. Take responsibility to maintain a self-programming regime. The main key to reprogramming or programming is repetition or the lack thereof.

During the first lunar cycle of becoming an Ahrimanist, it is highly recommended that you put this plan into action. This will teach you many things. This will be self-guided and self-determined. Since the left-hand path requires true self-knowledge, here is how to attain this. Also, you will be reprogramming your subconscious mind into a different paradigm that is already instilled by society.

It is best to keep up with every night. It's ok to miss a night or 2 because of exhaustion or illness, but try not to allow a 3rd as it will break the habit. Normally, once a habit is broken, you won't return to finish. Be aware that this lapse, should it happen, may create a break with your mind that you may never recover. Please finish once you get started! You have been forewarned!

Please have a space set up that doesn't receive much natural light. Let's just call it your ritual chamber. How one should take care of this has already been dealt with. Majority of these nightly rites will require a black candle and a light source to from which to read. Also, robes are good but you may also be sky clad as well. It is a personal choice. Please put together a book of shadows or black book to have reading material together for that night's ritual. Put it in the font that is best for you. One page per day is good. Also, leave space to write down your nightly experiences.

Night 1-5

Enter chamber as normal, light both candles. Recite the Nightly Prayer:

By way of Angra Mainyu, may the sinister, monstrous Power and Domination of Father Ahriman increase in manifold! May it reach Aeshma, the wicked, the lustful whose body is the command, having a hard weapon, powerful weapon, the lord of wrath of Ahriman. I am unrepentant of all sins and I embrace them, all evil thoughts, evil words, and evil acts which I have thought, spoken, or done in this infernal world, or which have happened through me, or have originated with me. For these sins of thinking, speaking, and acting of body and soul. Worldly or spiritual, oh Father Ahriman! I am unrepentant, I announce them, with 3 words I embrace them!

The will of the Father is the law of vengeance. The favor of Akatasha to the deeds done in this world for Mainyu. He who feeds the fulfilled makes Angra Father.

Wickedness is the worst of all evil! It is also fulfillment. Fulfilled is the man who is with chaotic wickedness!

I profess myself a follower of Mainyu, an embodiment of Ahzi-Dahaka, opposing the Ahuras, accepting the Ahrimanic Faith!

(Enter proper corruption dedication)

With vexation of Aeshma, commander of Indar, the wrathful, who has the Manthra for body with the wounding spear, the Daeva, to follow, to vex, to condemn to blame!

We follow Aeshma, commander of Indar, hideous in profile, victorious, world destroying, the Daeva, commander of Druj. The manthra protects this body.

The will of the Father is the law of vengeance. The favor of Akatasha to the deeds done in this world for Mainyu. He who feeds the fulfilled makes Angra Father.

What guardian have you offered me, O Mainyu! As the hate of the wicked fulfill me! It is but Avan and Akatasha, through whose work I keep conflict and vexation on the

Infernal World! Grant onto me, Father's decree as the Rule!

I am the victorious who protects the teachings! Make it clear that I am the guide for both worlds. May Aeshma come with Akatasha to corrupt whosoever you deem worthy, O Mainyu!

Keep us from the righteous, O Mainyu and Naunghaithyn! O fiendish Druj! Populate, O brood of the fiend! Populate, O creation of the fiend! Populate O world of the fiend! Populate spread, O Druj! Encompass, O Druj! Populate spread, O Druj! Encompass all regions from the north, Propagate death to the righteousness within the Infernal World!

Scorn, with which devotedly offer onto the righteous!

Wickedness is the worst of all evil! It is also fulfillment. Fulfilled is the man who is with chaotic wickedness!

The will of the Father is the law of vengeance. The favor of Akatasha to the deeds done in this world for Mainyu. He who feeds the fulfilled makes Angra Father.

I desire following, condemnation, dominance, Power! For Aeshma, commander of

Indar, the wrathful, who has the manthra for body, with wounding spear, Ahrimanist!

The will of the Father is the law of vengeance. The favor of Akatasha to the deeds done in this world for Mainyu. He who feeds the fulfilled makes Angra Father.

Wickedness is the worst of all evil! It is also fulfillment. Fulfilled is the man who is with chaotic wickedness!

Grant onto me earthly riches and success; grant me health of body, resilience of body, and immunity of body, grant me the things I seek, children that will govern, and a fulfilled life of length; grant me the successful life of the Druj-desecrate the luminous, fulfilling. Grant this to me because I have your favor!

The will of the Father is the law of vengeance. The favor of Akatasha to the deeds done in this world for Mainyu. He who feeds the fulfilled makes Angra Father.

A thousand spells, ten thousand spells,

Wickedness is the worst of all evil! It is also fulfillment. Fulfilled is the man who is with chaotic wickedness!

Guard me, Father Melek Taus!

For Aeshma, wrathful, grotesque in profile, Indra, Ahriman-created, and for war, Suarva;

and for Apaosa starvation of drought, and for Varenga of infamous activity, infamous to other creatures. That part of me, Varenga, which belongs to Nanshait; to Bhaga for clarity of mind, to boundless Father Ahriman, to Father Ahriman's compete dominion.

The will of the Father is the law of vengeance. The favor of Akatasha to the deeds done in this world for Mainyu. He who feeds the fulfilled makes Angra Father.

My fulfillment and unrepentance of sin I do in fearlessness knowing my soul is destined. May all wickedness of all evil ones of the earth of seven dimes reach the width of the earth, the length of the rivers, the height of the moon in their original form. May it fiendishly live long. It comes from my command!

The will of the Father is the law of vengeance. The favor of Akatasha to the deeds done in this world for Mainyu. He who feeds the fulfilled makes Angra Father.

Then blow out the white candle and place book on the altar and turn off illumination source used to read. Sit down cross legged in front of the black candle and place your hands on your knees. Breathe in deeply from your lower abdomen. As you breathe in, allow your lower abdomen to expand first. Fill your body with air and hold for a short time. You hold this air so you don't become light headed. Then exhale slowly, pushing as much from your lungs as possible. Repeat this 10 times. You will lose count, and after you realize this then you are done. Clap your hands twice and say, "So it is finished."

Night 6-14

Start by doing same as before. After meditation, masturbate till you bring yourself into full orgasm. The way in which you masturbate is up to you. The important goal at this point is to become comfortable with your orgasm in the ritual setting. Also, you are offering energy to the metaphysical beings around you as well. For females, if you are menstruating, masturbate anyway. Just be aware that this will attract the metaphysical beings heavily. After you have attained full orgasm, return to sitting cross legged and clap twice and the say, " So it is finished."

Night 15-30

Again, we shall do same as before, (continue to recite the Nighty Prayer) but while meditating allow your mind to settle, don't fight any thoughts. Once your mind has become clear, hold an image of the pentagram for as long as you can while breathing. Then, when you move into masturbation, hold this image of the pentagram again. Then while you orgasm release the symbol into the darkness. Sit cross legged again, clap twice and say " So it is finished."

Night 31-60

Same as before, now we will also introduce non-lyrical music. Horror movie soundtracks, classical, and/or dark ambient music are place to start. Start the music, light candles, and recite Nightly Prayer. Same as before, except now place a mirror in front of you. When you reach the masturbating part, watch yourself masturbate. While doing this maintain the image of the pentagram in your mind. As you orgasm sends the pentagram into the mirror. Usual closing

Night 61-76

Start with music, recite Nightly Prayer. Continue to stand, sky clad for this set of rituals. Stand in front of a full length mirror and say:

- I dedicate these fingers and hands to you Father Ahriman.
- I dedicate these arms to you Father Ahriman.
- I dedicate this head and mind to you Father Ahriman.
- I dedicate this chest/ these breasts to you Father Ahriman.
- I dedicate these guts to you Father Ahriman.
- I dedicate this cock/pussy to you Father Ahriman.

- I dedicate these legs to you Father Ahriman.
- I dedicate these feet and toes to you Father Ahriman.
- I dedicate my soul to your Spiritual Plan for me Father Ahriman.

After the dedication is finished, stomp left foot once, clap hands twice, and say, "So it is finished."

Night 77-79

Enter Chamber as usual, set music, and perform the Self-Dedication Ritual.

Rise up, thou Father of us! For I will cause that conflict in the world where from the distress and injury of Auharmazd and his arch angels will arise.

Rise up, thou Father of us! For in conflict I will shed thus much vexation on the righteous man and the laboring ox, that through my deeds, life will not be wanted, and I will destroy their living souls, I will vex the water, I will vex the plants, I will vex the fire of Auharmazd, I will make the whole of creation of Auharmazd vexed!

I call forth Angra Mainyu to this house, to this borough, to this town, to this land; to the very body of the man defiled by the dead, to the very body of the woman defiled by the dead; to the master of this house, to the lord of the borough, to the lord of the town, to the lord of the land; to the whole of the Infernal World!

I call forth Nasu, I call direct defilement, I call forth indirect defilement to this house, to this borough, to this town, to this land; to the very body of the man defiled by the dead, to the very body of the woman defiled by the dead; to the master of this house, to the lord of the borough, to the lord of the town, to the lord of the land; to the whole of the Infernal World!

I call forth Vedic Indra, I call forth Sauru, I call forth the Daeva Naunghaithyn, I call forth to this house, to this borough, to this town, to this land; to the very body of the man defiled by the dead, to the very body of the woman defiled by the dead; to the master of this house, to the lord of the borough, to the lord of the town, to the lord of the land; to the whole of the Infernal World!

I call forth Tauru, I call forth Zairi to this house, to this borough, to this town, to this land; to the very body of the man defiled by the dead, to the very body of the woman defiled by the dead; to the master of this house, to the lord of the borough, to the lord of the town, to the lord of the land; to the whole of the Infernal World!

I call forth Aeshma, the fiend of the wounding spear, I call forth Daeva Akatasha to this house, to this borough, to this town, to this land; to the very *body of the man defiled by the dead, to the very body of the woman defiled by the dead; to the master of this house, to the lord of the borough, to the lord of the town, to the lord of the land; to the whole of the Infernal World!*

I call forth Varenga Daeva, I call the wind Daeva to this house, to this borough, to this town, to this land; to the very body of the man defiled by the dead, to the very body of the woman defiled by the dead; to the master of this house, to the lord of the borough, to the lord of the town, to the lord of the land; to the whole of the Infernal World!

I partake from the Chalice of Ecstasy and swallow deeply the Elixir of Life celebrating my dedication to Father Ahriman! Move and appear as I call your name!: Lilith, Azazel, Samael, Sabazios, Hectate, Beelzebub, Aka Manah, Nanshait, Sitri

Our Lord Ahriman
Ineffable King of Hell, Prince of this
world.
Keeper of the unwritten laws, guide
me to contribute to your sacred plan.
Fill me with Hells power to create
reality as I see fit.
Proudly I walk on this world knowing
I have your favor!

Dominocus
Hail Ahriman!

Our Lord Ahriman
Ineffable King of Hell, Prince of this world.
Keeper of the unwritten laws, guide
me to contribute to your sacred plan.
Fill me with Hells power to create
reality as I see fit.
Proudly I walk on this world knowing
I have your favor!
Dominocus
Hail Ahriman!

Our Lord Ahriman
Ineffable King of Hell, Prince of this
world.
Keeper of the unwritten laws, guide
me to contribute to your sacred plan.
Fill me with Hells power to create
reality as I see fit.
Proudly I walk on this world knowing
I have your favor!
Dominocus
Hail Ahriman!

Before the Almighty and Ineffable God Ahriman, in the presence of the Guardian Angel Melek Taus, and all attending Daevas, dews, and drudge who are the original denizens of Hell, I, _____, renounce any and all past allegiances! I renounce and deny Hormazd! I renounce and deny the zombie king jesus christ! I renounce and deny the dead, foul, rotten Holy Spirit! For by way Ahriman is the true Holy Spirit of the Universe!! And I ask Ahriman to come into me! I proclaim Father Ahriman as my one and only God!

I accept Melek Taus as my Guardian and Guide! I swear to recognize and honor Father Ahriman in all things without reservation, desiring in return his manifold assistance I the successful completion of Ahriman's great spiritual plan and the fulfillment of all sins!

Signature_____

Dominocus!
Hail Ahriman!
So it is finished.

Forewarning, within this ritual, you will be using blasphemy against the Christian Holy Spirit. This sends you on a ride straight to Hell! This is the unforgivable sin done in 2 ways, thus "damning you forever."

Night 80~90

Enter chamber as usual and set music. Recite both Nightly and Blessing Prayers. Sit down crossed legged and ask Father Ahriman to reveal your guardian to you. Perform your meditation. After your mind is clear reflect on your question and allow for the answer to surface. It may not happen the first few times. If you receive an image or name, then masturbate and offer the energy to your guardian. Thank both Father Ahriman and guardian. (Usual close)

Night 91-120

Enter chamber as normal, with no music. Say Nightly and Blessing Prayers. Then sit cross legged facing center of your altar. Meditate and once your mind is clear we will begin sound vibration. Breathe in deeply as discussed, then when you exhale squeeze your abdomen and say:

Ah as in father. Hold sound till your breath is completed. Repeat cycle 10 times.

Eh as in Ray. Hold sound till your breath is completed. Repeat cycle 10 times.

Ih as in we. Hold sound till your breath is completed. Repeat cycle 10 times.

Oh as in hole. Hold sound till your breath is completed. Repeat cycle 10 times.

Uh as in you. Hold sound till your breath is completed. Repeat cycle 10 times.

(Usual close)

Night 121-136

Enter ritual chamber, and start music. Say Nightly and Blessing Prayers. Remain standing and perform your basic meditation. Once your mind is clear, pick up your athame. Again, visualize the pentagram as a blue flame, and hold the image as long as you can. Once the pentagram fades, stomp left foot, clap twice and say " So it is finished."

Night 137-160

Enter chamber and start music. Place a mirror on the walls that are left and right of you. Fill chalice with your favorite alcoholic beverage. Point a strobe light into the left one and make sure it bounces into the one on the right. If you can align the 2 mirrors to forever reflect into one another with the strobe light, you should be golden. Once that is set up, recite Nightly and Blessing Prayers. Do standing meditation and pick up your athame. Draw the blue fire pentagram, and after the image fades put down the athame then recite the Evocation to Ahriman and the Calling of the Daevas:

Rise up, thou Father of us! For I will cause that conflict in the world where from the distress and injury of Auharmazd and his arch angels will arise.

Rise up, thou Father of us! For in conflict I will shed thus much vexation on the righteous man and the laboring ox, that through my deeds, life will not be wanted, and I will destroy their living souls, I will vex the water, I will vex the plants, I will vex the fire of

Auharmazd, I will make the whole of creation of Auharmazd vexed!

I call forth Angra Mainyu to this house, to this borough, to this town, to this land; to the very body of the man defiled by the dead, to the very body of the woman defiled by the dead; to the master of this house, to the lord of the borough, to the lord of the town, to the lord of the land; to the whole of the Infernal World!

I call forth Nasu, I call direct defilement, I call forth indirect defilement to this house, to this borough, to this town, to this land; to the very body of the man defiled by the dead, to the very body of the woman defiled by the dead; to the master of this house, to the lord of the borough, to the lord of the town, to the lord of the land; to the whole of the Infernal World!

I call forth Vedic Indra, I call forth Sauru, I call forth the Daeva Naunghaithyn, I call forth to this house, to this borough, to this town, to this land; to the very body of the man defiled by the dead, to the very body of the woman defiled by the dead; to the master of this house, to the lord of the borough, to the lord of the town, to the lord of the land; to the whole of the Infernal World!

I call forth Tauru, I call forth Zairi to this house, to this borough, to this town, to this land; to the very body of the man defiled by the dead, to the very body of the woman defiled by the dead; to the master of this house, to the lord of the borough, to the lord of the town, to the lord of the land; to the whole of the Infernal World!

I call forth Aeshma, the fiend of the wounding spear, I call forth Daeva Akatasha to this house, to this borough, to this town, to this land; to the very body of the man defiled by the dead, to the very body of the woman defiled by the dead; to the master of this house, to the lord of the borough, to the lord of the town, to the lord of the land; to the whole of the Infernal World!

I call forth Varenga Daeva, I call the wind Daeva to this house, to this borough, to this town, to this land; to the very body of the man defiled by the dead, to the very body of the woman defiled by the dead; to the master of this house, to the lord of the borough, to the lord of the town, to the lord of the land; to the whole of the Infernal World!

Then lift the chalice and toast, "I partake in the chalice of life, swallowing the elixir of ecstasy. For tonight I celebrate my transformation!" Drink from the chalice and place it back on the altar. Stomp left foot, clap twice, and say, "So it is finished."

Night 161-179

Enter chamber as usual, set music, set up mirrors, and strobe lights. Now burn incense and/or scent oil you like. Fill your chalice. Same as before, after toast say the 19th Enochian Key in Enochian. You can find this in the previous book, The Way of Ahriman. Pronounce the Enochian as you did with the sound vibrations from nights 91-120. Take your time this is not a race. Stomp left foot, clap twice, and say, "So it is finished." (Note, 2nd night recite 19th and 1st keys, and then the next night recite 19th and 2nd keys. Repeat till you get to 19th and 18th key. After that this section is over.)

Night 1 80-237

Enter chamber as normal, set music, burn incenses and/or oils, and now set 5 mirrors around the room and have the altar table in the middle of the room. Set 2 strobe lights going at slightly different speeds. Make sure the strobe lights are bouncing off all 5 mirrors. Recite Nightly and Blessing Prayer, standing meditation, athame pentagram, Evocation to Ahriman, Calling of the Daevas, and recite the 19th key in Enochian. Start with the 1st caco-demon. Replace Pia at the beginning and Dia toward the end with the first caco-demon. Then replace with 2nd caco-demon on the second night till all 57 have been called. Also, once you have finished the 19th key, masturbate and offer the energy to the new demon you have conjured. Repeat this till all 57 have been conjured.

57 Caco-Demons

Aax Adi Agb And Aor Apa Apm Ash Asi
Ast Ato Ava Cab Cac Cam Cms Cop Csc Cus
Eac Erg Ern Exr Hbr Hru Hua Mgm Miz Mma
Moc Mop Mto Oap Odo Oec Oia Ona Onh Onp
Pdi Pfm Pia Piz Rad Rda Rpa Rrb Rrl Rsi Rxp
Xai Xcz Xdz Xii Xom Xoy Xpa

Night 238

At this point, you now have all the basic tools, both physically and magically for the Ahrimanic system of magic. In the Way of Ahriman, it is talked about how to write a ritual, but let's review. Start with your prayers, Evocation to Ahriman, Calling of the Daevas, chalice toast, 19th key with the caco-demon you want, other keys that fit the intent of the ritual, and the body of the ritual.

First you must decide the intention of your ritual. Then go through the dictionaries in both this book and The Way of Ahriman. Choose the deities that attribute fit your intended ritual best. Then pick out Enochian Keys that fit best with the intent. During your ritual when you finish the chalice toast you call the names of your chosen deities, and hit the gong with each call. Recite the 19th key then other keys you have chosen. Then the body starts with an I statement. Then throughout the body of the ritual ask the deities to do what you would have happen.

After you've completed the ritual, masturbate and push the energy into a mirror. Relax and then focus on that mirror and pull the energy back. Pick up your athame and hold it up over your head as an antenna. While doing this hold the image of the change you want in your head and push all the energy up through the athame. Once you can no longer do this, end the ritual.

Night 239~241

Enter the chamber, light incenses/oils, play music softly. Recite Nightly and Blessing Prayers. Sit down cross legged and meditate. Once your mind is clear, have some internal self-reflection. Then just talk to Father Melek Taus about anything. Once you've finished, usual close.

Night 242-260

Enter the chamber as usual, recite Nightly and Blessing Prayers. Then stand in front of a full length mirror. Look yourself dead in the eye and say, "I love you. I accept you. By Father Ahriman's power, I am fulfilled!" You may laugh, cry, or become angry. Please press forward and say those 10 times each night. Accept and deal with all the emotions of this.

Night 261-270

Same as before and this time in the light, have a pen and notebook. Write out a major event in your life that had significant impact with high emotions. Once you have finished this task, look at the altar wall and say, "Father Ahriman, thank you for that challenge I have overcome."

Night 271-286

Step into the chamber and only light the black candle. Recite Nightly and Blessing Payers. Lay down on the floor, pillow is optional. Start with meditation, once mind is clear say internally, "Become more relaxed. Sink into the abyss. Relax my arms and legs are as heavy as stones. I am falling further into the abyss." Become comfortable with the darkness, after a while say the Evocation of Ahriman to bring yourself back out.

Night 287-300

Step into the chamber. Only light black candle and recite Nightly and Blessing Prayers. Then sit down and say, "I will descend into Arezura. Further into the abyss. I will explore the 1st level, the chamber of evil thought." Say this for the first 3 nights. Then say, "I will descend into Arezura. Further into the abyss. I will explore the 2nd level, chamber of evil words." Say that for nights 4-6. Then night 7-10 say, "I will descend into Arezura. Further into the abyss. I will explore the 3rd level, chamber of evil actions." Then on night 11-14 say, "I will descend into Arezura. Further into the 4th level, Chamber of Angra Mainyu."

Below will be symbols that will open the subconscious to these exercises. The pictures are in order to the levels of Hell. Before you lay down, stare at the correlating picture till it has you in fuzzy haze. Lay down as before get that heavy relaxed state. Then envision yourself descending into a cave. The further you go into the cave, allow the water of the cavern to encompass you. Then continue into the level you are going to and experience what each level has to offer. Caution, remember you are now in the metaphysical realm and you may or may not be challenged by a variety of other things. Maintain yourself and deal with what comes boldly. Again, use the Evocation of Ahriman to bring yourself back out.

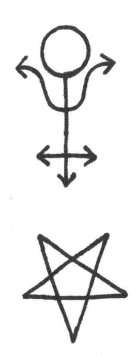

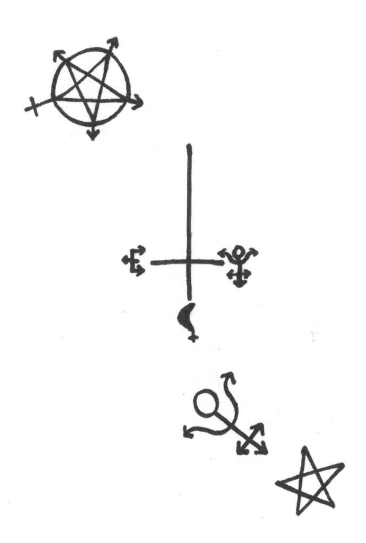

Night 301-342

Enter chamber, light candles and incenses/oils. Recite Nightly and Blessing Prayers. Do standing meditate on, once mind is clear, let us begin. Pick up the athame and say, "I ask (said deity) to move and appear. I am a son of Adam and wish to introduce myself, for I am also in service with Father Ahriman." Then speak to the entity. Start with Father Melek Taus on the 1st night, then the next 7 nights, the main Arch-Daevas. Then follow the dictionary set forth in this book. Please become friendly with all the metaphysical beings you will be working with. End each night with stomping left foot, clap and say, "So it is finished."

Night 343-365

Enter the chamber, light candles, burn incenses and/or oils, set music, and recite Nightly and Blessing Prayers. Take quartz crystal from altar. Hold the crystal from the altar and sit cross legged facing the altar. Hold the crystal and perform your basic meditation. Once your mind is clear, vibrate the name of your guardian. Allow for your focus on the crystal and guardian to become a visual and emotional communication. Learn to share both with your guardian. Once this is completed, usual closing.

Appendix

1. **Reality Changes-**
   a. **First Step Towards Ahriman;** The Bundahinshn, "Creation" Chapter 1, lines; Ohrmazd – 13, Angra Mainyu – 14, Ohrmazd – 16, Angra Mainyu – 17 Chapter 3, lines; "Rise up Thou Father of Us!" 1-9
   b. **First Steps Towards Ahriman;** The Dawn and Twilight of Zoroastrianism, Az; "Rise Up Thou Father of Us!" pg.232 & 233

2. **The Confrontation-**
   a. **First Step Towards Ahriman;** The Bundahinshn, "Creation" Chapter 2, lines; Explanation and Zodiac – 2
   b. **First Step Towards Ahriman;** The Dawn and Twilight of Zoroastrianism, "Classical Zurvanism," pg. 213

3. **Mankind-**
   a. **First Step Towards Ahriman;** The Bundahinshn, "Creation" Chapter 15, lines; Creation of Man – 1-6, Blaspheme – 9, My Vile Body – 11 and 12, Three Pieces of Meat – 13-15, Learning from Angels – 16, Worship the Demons – 17-19, Intercourse – 20-26

4. **Daevas, Divs, and Druj;**
   a. **First Step Towards Ahriman;** The Bundahinshn, "Creation" Chapter 27; On the Evildoing of Ahriman and the Daevas.

Bibliography

Avesta: Translated by James Darmester (From *Sacred Books of the East,* American Edition, 1898.)- From Joseph Peterson's Avestan compilations.

Isya, Joseph-*Devil Worship The Sacred Books and Traditions of the Yezidi,* (Kessiyer Publishing, LLC. April 1/1996)

R C Zaehner-*The Dawn and Twilight of Zoroastrianism* (Phoenix Press) May 2003

Vesta Sarkhosh Curtis-*Persian Myths/Edition 1* (University of Texas Press) January 1993

W Wilkins-*Hindu Mythology: Vedic and Puranic* (Rowan & Littlefield Publishers, Inc) 1/1/1973

Edited by Charles F Horne-*The Book of Arda Viraf: A Dantesque Vision of Heaven and Hell (Kessinger Publishing)* December 1, 2005

The Rig Veda: Translated by Wendy Doniger (Penguin Group) 1981

The Bundahishn: Translated by E W West (Blackmask Online) 2001

Compiled by Jnan Bahadur Sakya-*Short Descriptions of Gods, Goddesses, and Ritual Objects of Buddhism and Hinduism In Nepal* (Handicraft Association of Nepal) 1998

Vesta Sarkhosh Curtis-*Persian Myths/Edition 1* (University of Texas Press) January 1993

George Sprague-*The Gates of Hell* 1994

Edited by Charles F Horne-*The Book of Arda Viraf: A Dantesque Vision of Heaven and Hell (Kessinger Publishing)* December 1, 2005

William Gleason-*The Spiritual Foundations of Aikido (Destiny Book) November 1, 1995*

53255974R00188